Tibetan Reflections

Tibetan Reflections

Life in a Tibetan Refugee Community

Peter Gold

Photographs by the Author

Illustrations by Tibetan Artists

Introduction by Thubten Jigme Norbu

Wisdom Publications

Illustrations

Pen and ink drawings by Tibetan artist
Lobsang Tendzin (courtesy of the William H. Mathers
Museum of Indiana University)
Woodblock prints by anonymous Tibetan artists
Photographs by Peter Gold,
except facing page 32 by Hiroki Fujita.

Cover photograph of prayer flags by Peter Gold
Cover designed by Humphrey Stone
Photograph of the author by Jw Ramsey

First published in 1984

Wisdom Publications
PO Box 4BJ, London W1
and
Conishead Priory
Ulverston, Cumbria
England

© Peter Gold 1984

ISBN 0 86171 022 3

Designed by Humphrey Stone

Set in Palatino 12 on 15 point
by Characters of Chard, Somerset
and printed and bound in
Singapore by Eurasia Press

Contents

Acknowledgments

This collection of essays issued from three sojourns with Tibetans living in the foothills of the Indian Himalayas. I would like to thank my many Tibetan friends in India, as well as friends of Tibet in the West, for their advice and help in realizing this book.

Through the aid of the National Endowment for the Arts and Indiana University I journeyed to the mile-high town of Dharamsala, home of eight thousand Tibetans and their spiritual and political leader, His Holiness the Fourteenth Dalai Lama. Tibetan social, religious, and artistic traditions hang on in this borderland aerie, scarcely fifty miles from Tibet as the crow flies.

A generation has passed since the Tibetans' sad exodus from their homeland. Despite unmentionable hardships encountered as refugees, their enthusiasm and impetus for living in a world which they view as imperfect yet full of enormous potential, have kept them fit and distinctly Tibetan. In turn the Tibetan way has continued to capture the imagination of the Western world, serving as an inspiration to us all.

Bloomington, Indiana
February 1982

Introduction

This book presents a view of the Tibetan way of life through the eyes of an experienced Western observer.

Peter Gold has spent eight months living in the company of Tibetans in India, studying our religion, arts and language. He has distilled these experiences into words in order to portray the facts and feeling of Tibetan life. The result is one that non-Tibetans may readily appreciate.

In this entertaining book one comes to know Tibetans as individuals, as down to earth people, living more like yourself and your neighbors than like inhabitants of some exotic *Shangri-la*.

I hope the reader will enjoy *Tibetan Reflections*. It is also my hope that it will further aid the understanding of what it means to be Tibetan.

THUBTEN JIGME NORBU
February, 1982

A First Word

In the pre-dawn light the eyes must strain to discern the contours of houses, prayer flags and wooded hills. In the effort, the realness of the place and its people becomes elusive, and the question of its very existence unfolds as the subject of a dialogue before the mind.

Dharamsala is a special intersection of time and place.

Within a mere generation former dwellers of the snows and dizzying heights have made the great leap downward into this crazy world. Eighty thousand Tibetans climbed, slipped and scrambled across mountain vastnesses and icy passes, down to the very edge of the lowlands, steamy jungles by comparison.

Dharamsala is one of the most Tibet-like of their many settlements in India. The folk here rest poised on a slowly moving balance, one foot in either world, as it measures out the fate of their culture. Tenaciously they hang from the rocky slopes finding time to give birth, pray, play and die, as they live out the human game with all its faults and favors.

Here the ancient ways are preserved. They swirl about in a dramatic *pas de deux* with those of the mish-mash world below, like oil in water. The culture of Tibet — last of a brood of untouched ancient civilizations — hangs on delicately, but with great momentum and determination. The tiny town of Dharamsala has developed broad nerve fibers that reach out past immediate Indian villages and cities, out over the subcontinent, and across oceans, mountain ranges, and deserts to connect with the world beyond.

In the process the place has become more than a simple union of people and land. It has entered the realm of ideas. Perhaps it is this aspect that I am enabled to grasp by the shifting light of the coming dawn.

Part I Linking up

Incense

"They will have an incense-burning ceremony on Wednesday morning," two Tibetan friends informed me. "You mustn't miss it."

Incense is a favored form of offering the world over. It effectively satisfies two senses: that of smell and, by its smoke, that of sight.

Incense is enigmatic to our classificatory minds. We sense it yet it remains intangible, elusive. The smoke is visible for a few moments, seemingly real. Yet it is no longer traceable when dispersed sufficiently into the air. We know it still exists, somewhere, but it no longer fits that conventional category of "really existing" that our mind's experience wishes to ascribe to it.

As the smoke ascends vertically and disperses among the molecules of air, our individual spirits are joined metaphorically with the sky and its implied infinity beyond.

Tibetan incense comes in bundles of thin brownish sticks about sixteen inches in length. Incense such as this was what I had expected to see burning at what Tibetans call *sangsu*, the ceremonial offering of burned fragrances. Given the Tibetans' love of ritual drama and their predilection for naturally-occurring objects as sources of their symbols, I was soon to realize that this ceremony involved more than a few sticks of incense.

The *sangsu* took place at a small shrine ground on

12

Giving offerings of fragrant evergreen smoke to the host of Buddhas and all sentient beings. The sangsu *ceremony is held before the shrine to the fierce protector-goddess of the Tibetan people,* Palden Lhamo. *The monks chant the liturgy while the assembled worshippers follow along having placed their offerings of specially-prepared incense into the fire.*

the side of the hilltop upon which sit the main temple and palace of the Dalai Lama. Its small stone and earthen buildings are repositories of *tsa-tsa*, offerings of molded clay and paper bearing *mantras*. Overlooking the offering ground is the main shrine, the *lhaptsi*, dedicated to *Palden Lhamo*, the wrathful looking protector-goddess of the Tibetan people. They lie along the *lingkhor*, the route of circumambulation, a well-beaten stony and earthen path skirting the mountainside. Here, by their walking action, worshipers link up with the power of the Buddha and his many manifestations. They gain karmic merit in the process by chanting their *mantras* to the count of rosary beads, and by leaving offerings on stone cairns all along the way.

The clockwise walk along the *lingkhor* is formidable not only for its scenic beauty — the Kangra Valley stretches endlessly below — but for the implied power

13

emanating from the offerings lining the rocky path, physical evidence of concentrated human expression engaged in spiritual contract.

The offerings vary with the whims of the individuals making them. Mini-mountains of conical piles of gray stones, topped by others — some white and crystalline — seem to have grown in place, right out of the rocky earth. Pine boughs punctuate the almost abstract-expressionist, stone constructions. They remind one of miniature megaliths from bygone days blending back into the foliage and soil. Likewise, incised *mani* stone palettes bearing *mantras* such as *om mani padme hung*, lie nonchalantly atop and below the stone cairns, in the crooks of tree limbs along the path, on rocky ledges, on grassy knolls, and on top of countless other *mani* stones. Pieces of cloth, shocks of human hair, and prayer strings blessed by lamas hang significantly from branches of brambles. These, too, are offerings to the deities and all thinking and feeling beings, whom Tibetans know to exist within their own earthly space as well as in the realms of the sky and underworld.

The act of walking along in the crystalline morning light, the experience of seeing all these physical offerings and the hovering implication of their placement mingled in my mind with the dawning awareness of a sweet aroma in the air. It all created an overwhelmingly pleasant conceptual brew.

We were now almost upon the shrine site and already it was apparent that this was not the delicate smell of Tibetan stick incense but the more pungent, yet equally favorable scent of burning pine needles. And I remembered the Tibetans' reverence for the evergreen as incense, stimulant, and symbol of the verticality of the universe, indeed life itself. The tree, like the mountain, metaphysically unites through its verticality the three realms of the cosmos: sky, earth, and under-the-earth.

Palden Lhamo, *the wrathful blue-skinned protector-goddess of Tibet. Her image adorns the ceremonial room of the main temple and is enshrined in a special enclosure at the site of the monthly ceremony of burned fragrances. She is depicted riding an ass, with human skulls and skins dangling from the saddle, symbols of her power and of life's impermanence.*

It is only fitting then that this ceremony both express the wish for the long life of His Holiness the Dalai Lama, their spiritual tree, staff of their lives, and serve as a communal act of entering into spiritual contact and contract with the Buddha, gods, protectors, and those spirits inhabiting the less desirable realms of this multileveled universe.

It is also fitting that these offerings be morticed by the incense of the evergreen, no longer juniper since it is not abundant here in the Himalayan foothills, but pine, which is evergreen, ever-living, fully-manifesting life.

On coming around the final bend in the *lingkhor* my eyes were greeted by an intense cloud of white, opalescent smoke. The source of the mysterious fragrance, it billowed skyward like a tree, carrying prayers of the assembled people into the sky. It seemed that the prayers remained in our earthly realm for as long as the smoke remained corporeal as an ascending vortex.

15

When it dispersed among the molecules of air, however, one could not help feeling that the prayers had entered the realm of the infinite.

A large stone urn provided the hearth for the burning of perhaps an entire tree's worth of pine boughs. The fire provided the physical heat energy for the smoky message. The spiritual energy was fueled by successive individuals emptying embroidered bags of their contents of *sang*, specially-prepared juniper needle incense, into the fire. *Tsamba*, roasted barley flour, rice by the handful, and draughts of *chang*, Tibetan grain beer, completed the offering fare.

Prayer flags were newly raised for the occasion, and fluttered in the morning sky. They joined hundreds of other previously offered red, blue, yellow, white and green flags. Each was printed with *mantras* and salutations to various deities to be multiplied thousands of times daily as they fluttered in the wind. This rainbow of colored light carried their requests to the fountain of the infinite, for the benefit of all thinking and feeling beings.

White gauzey *khatag* scarves, traditional means of greeting and offering, were hung upon the prayer plaque on the front of the shrine. First they would be baptized in the smoke. Then, after forming a *mantra* or prayer on their lips, the offerants would fling the *khatag* upon the power place of *Palden Lhamo*.

The *chang* bottles, still containing most of their liquids, and piles of *tsamba* were then carried to the low dais set before a line of chanting monks and lay persons. These would be given by the monks to the fire on everyone's behalf. The people then joined the rest of us behind the official party, in a grove of pines and rhododendron trees, facing the altar with our backs to the valley floor spreading far below.

The chants continued without stop. The people gave their offerings to the fire and shrine as they arrived.

Some proceeded to sit down, others circumambulated the attendant shrines.

The chants swirled on. They were offerings in the form of sound. They resounded off the hillside and rose into the air like the smoke.

The chants flowed on. Handfuls of roasted barley flour, liquor droplets, spinning prayer wheels, *mantras*, personal prayers, fluttering prayer flags, *khatag* scarves, and the smoke all served as prayer-bearing offerings.

When the prayers were completed and the offerings given, all rose to their feet. *En masse*, the owners retrieved their *chang* bottles, now decidedly empty. Raising the bottles into the air as if to show that the offerings were a success, they rejoined the others at the edge of the hill.

A huge semi-circle of people faced the altar area. Seemingly on cue, an inspired old warrior dressed in an ancient *chuba* cloak covered with a modern down jacket, burst into the empty amphitheatre and launched into a high pitched, Tibetan victory song.

His impassioned delivery, punctuated by stylized chevron-like arm and body gestures, was soon joined by everyone present and became a stirring means of group solidarity.

By this time everyone held *tsamba* powder in their upraised right hands. A sense of togetherness and common purpose permeated the crowd. The song completed, we offered a toast to the gods in loud glissando voices: *tso* (I offer) *tso, tso, lha, gyal lo* (victory to the gods!). And, into the air and onto each other we tossed our barley flour, the sacred symbol of Tibet much as corn is for the American Indian. Gods and people thus fulfilled, we departed for home.

The Golden Buddha by the Sacred Juniper

The Buddha of our present era, Shakyamuni, spent long years in quest of enlightenment. After many trials and worldly experiences he finally succeeded. This woodblock print depicts Buddha in the state of enlightened meditation. His left hand is in the mudra *(gesture) of meditation, his right in the earth-touching* mudra, *signifying the earth as a witness to his attainment of enlightenment. This image serves Tibetans as a clear reminder of the ultimate goal of Buddhist practice.*

There is a lone juniper tree atop one of the highest ridge tops in Dharamsala. Junipers, cousins to our own eastern red cedars, are quite rare here, and this one is the more remarkable considering its advanced age. It grows at the northwest corner of the great temple of the Tibetan Buddhists in India, sharing the same grounds as the palace of His Holiness the Dalai Lama.

It is four p.m. and the winter sun is very strong, welcomingly, even oppressively, hot in this clear lapis blue sky. I am also a juniper. Green with the life and spirit of this place and its people. I am not as aged as this tree but I am beginning to show my age. I am firmly planted at this moment on the veranda at the southeast corner of the temple, equally a silent sentinel with ever-deepening roots.

People circumambulate the temple clockwise, as is the custom of the Tibetan Buddhists, centering their minds as they circle this place of power. The sun, also a circle to the natural eye, shines down upon the circle of walkers. Circumambulation completes the walker's meditative act and signifies the attainment of one more unit of positive, spiritual wealth.

Inside the circle of pilgrims, the temple radiates its own kind of energy, focused by the huge gold and brass Buddha which the Tibetans invest with a power similar to that of the sun.

I have been here twice in the sun, on the sacred hill under the golden Buddha by the sacred juniper. Once with mind dazzled by all that was strange and unknown, and again today drawn here it seems for no reason at all. Both times the sublimity of the place has quieted me, softened that edge which sometimes envelops me.

Here is a place containing contrasts that are exaggerated by its powerful sublimity. A sudden stranger from the other side of the earth, I am now descended upon by a group of chattering Indian tourists. Photos! Photos! I am also in the company of monks, nuns, and circumambulating *ama-las*, those delightful old Tibetan ladies one sees everywhere with checkered toothy grins, brown weathered skin, homespun black wool *chubas*, and ever-spinning prayer wheels. Their children and grandchildren all grown, with time on their hands the *ama-las* and their mates the *pa-las* now have the opportunity to enter fully into spiritual activities to actively improve their *karma* in preparation for their future lives.

Here, at this moment it is as if I am viewing a TV set both from the non-committal comfort of my easy chair and simultaneously from within the tube as an actor in a very real drama.

I am with an *ama-la*. I watch her, scarcely ten feet from me, take off her shoes, put the large *mala* rosary around her neck, and gently lay down her prayer wheel and scarf on the yellow offering box outside the glassy temple doors. Murmuring numerous *om mani padme hungs* and other appropriate *mantras* and prayers, she kneels and performs a complete prostration extending her body upon a quilted pad set on the hard stone floor. *Ama-la* is a blur of black, brown, turquoise and colored stripes as she surrenders before the source of her devotion.

Over and over again, in the same motions: clasped hands touching head, throat and heart, knees bend-

ing, forehead touching the earth, arms stretching out in front, sphinx-like. As the arms fully extend, the rest of the body follows until it becomes one with the earth. Then all returns to the beginning in reverse motion, to cycle over scores of times.

It is a powerful faith that motivates the *ama-las'* and *pa-las'* complete offering of themselves. Although it is an offering to deities, ultimately it is a means of personal growth. By giving one's energy through devoted and intense concentration one ultimately gains in a process that Buddhists call accumulating positive merit.

Among speedy-minded Westerners, such sustained concentration and mindful attention is very rare indeed. And when we participate in it, it rarely matches the half an hour of intense yogic calisthenics performed by this aged woman.

The quilted pad on which she offers her body and mind to the Buddha without and within has slowly, imperceptibly moved forward with her constant prostrating motion. And it seems as if there has developed an almost visible bond, a psychic cord between the top of her head and the glowing golden statue of the Buddha just visible beyond the glass doors, shimmering in the light of the setting sun.

Suddenly I get an impulse to lay down my scribbling pencil and join her. Yet, just as I register this thought, she ends her prostrations, picks up her devotional objects, and enters the temple to come face to face with the golden Buddha statue, symbolizing the desire for enlightenment that is infusing her mind.

The sun is rapidly setting now. *Ama-la* is still inside the temple offering energy and receiving it back multifold. I too feel fulfilled and content. That anxious feeling that I brought with me from the other side of the world is slowly losing its grip. Today, here, high on a hill in the lap of the Himalayas bathed in golden light, sitting among devoted souls as eagles glide below snowy peaks, anxiety finds no foundation and is gone!

Sunbeams in the Drizzle

Kalsang Tharghey, my exuberant Tibetan companion, repeatedly beckoned me out of the drizzle toward the restaurant.

But something was keeping me out in the cold, dripped upon from the run-off of a shop's roof on the main street in McLeod Ganj, the Tibetans' village in Dharamsala.

It was rapidly approaching dusk and the usual bazaar sounds merged into a many-textured symphony. Tea glasses clinked to Lhasa Apsos' barks. Conversations in the melodious Tibetan language formed an obligato to the clang of the bell marking the completed rotation of a huge prayer wheel filled with offerings of countless *mantras*. And the whisping, whirring, spinning banks of smaller, bronze prayer wheels were counterpointed by the harmony of chanted *om mani padme hungs* from the lips of worshipers giving up these offerings on behalf of all thinking and feeling beings as they circumambulated the holy *stupa*. All these sounds flooded my ears.

But there was something else keeping me out in the rain. The usual throng of people crowded the busy street that leads to what used to be a summer residence of the British Raj and now ends at the temple and palace of the Dalai Lama. But tonight its ambience seemed somehow different, a difference reflected in the eager glances in the direction of the Dalai Lama's palace and in the appearance of scores of lighted bundles of stick incense. It was then that I remembered that His Holiness was due to depart on an India-wide tour of Tibetan settlements sometime this very day. So, the word was out. His motor entourage would soon pass this way.

This was the undefinable ambience that was keeping me out in the rain; the collective expectation and well-wishing of these people had made itself unconsciously felt. When the maroon Mercedes, like a queen bee amongst a host of worker jeeps made its appearance, incense sticks, clasped hands, heads and shoulders leaned reverently forward in unison, as if stout, young saplings bent in a firm but gentle gale.

I took my hat from my head and held it to my chest, at first self-consciously, but this feeling quickly passed as I abandoned my inhibitions, overcome by the oneness of the moment. It feels good to let the heart do the thinking from time to time.

A Place of Power

On leaving the palace grounds and the Dalai Lama after his New Year blessing, I found myself in the middle of devotional activities centering about the temple.

The temple is situated upon the hill alongside the Dalai Lama's palace. Together they surge with an invisible energy that even the dullest of minds cannot fail to acknowledge.

The Dalai Lama is the human emanation of the *bodhisattva Chenrezi (Avalokiteshvara)*, a saint who embodies the boundlessly compassionate aspect of the Buddha's consciousness. In a similar way, the temple's holy relics, consecrated *thangkas*, statues, scriptures and implements are, for the devoted, the earthly material manifestations of the infinite and liberated mind field which is Buddha. The huge statues of the Buddha, the thousand-armed *Chenrezi*, and *Padmasambhava*, the Indian tantric master who introduced Buddhism into Tibet in a way that made it harmonious with the pre-existing beliefs, are holy and powerful objects. For Tibetans, they are imbued with the same liberated mind energy as was Gautama Buddha, and is the Dalai Lama.

It is no wonder then that the throngs of people having just been blessed by a human manifestation of the Buddha, should now wish to circumambulate the temple, prostrate before it, meditate beside it, walk respectfully through it or simply be within the vicinity of it.

There are likewise other power places here in Dharamsala and many people frequently make the rounds to each. The most devout, or those with ample time on their hands, make their rounds daily.

Below the palace and temple grounds people amble along the *lingkhor*, the offering trail. Many continue onto the bazaar at McLeod Ganj, where they repeat these offerings around the *stupa*. Like the conical hills on which the palace and temple are situated, the *stupa* is a mountain-like construction solid in foundation, conical in form, forceful in vertical momentum, and imbued with spiritual power through consecration and belief.

People circumambulate the *stupa*, which is topped with a golden moon, sun and jewel, and turn prayer wheels arranged in banks along either side of it. The prayer wheels at the *stupa*, like those swung in the hands of the devout, contain hundreds of thousands of printed *Chenrezi* mantras, *om mani padme hung*,

Sample of printed mantra *sheets, which are wound onto rolls for inclusion within the hand-held prayer wheel,* mani khor. *By spinning the wheel countless times daily and invoking the* mantras *included within, one compounds each chanted invocation by a factor consisting of the number of printed prayers, multiplied by the number of revolutions of the wheel. An enormous amount of merit is thus accumulated towards happiness in this and future lifetimes.*

ཨ་དྷ་ཧེ་སྡེ་ནོ་ཧ་པོ་སྡེ་ནོ་ཧ་བ་དྷེ་སྡེ་ནོ་ཧ་དྷེ་སྡེ་ནོ་ཧ་བ་པ་སྡེ་ནོ་ཧ་དྷེ་སྡེ་ནོ་ཧ་

ཨ་དྷ་སྡེ་ནོ་ཧ་པོ་སྡེ་ནོ་ཧ་བ་དྷེ་སྡེ་ནོ་ཧ་དྷེ་སྡེ་ནོ་ཧ་བ་པ་སྡེ་ནོ་ཧ་

which multiply their vocalized prayers that number of times with each revolution of the wheel.

To cap the *stupa* experience a person may choose to spin the huge prayer wheel situated in the shrine house adjacent to the *stupa*. Like the smaller prayer wheel it magnifies their prayerful offerings, only more so. Like an electrical transformer it amplifies their individual inputs into the universal power circuit, hooking them securely into the totality of things.

With a philosophy so vast and infinite in scope as Buddhism, it is understandable that Tibetans would wish to deal in such vast numerical multiplications of spirituality.

It is also fitting that they do so with the most ancient of motions, the circular and the vertical. The circle is infinite in its completeness and indivisibility, while the vertical plane is equally infinite in its immeasurability.

The very act of circular movement around a spiri-

Map of the Tibetan universe showing the four-sided cosmic mountain, rirab lhungpo, *at the center, surrounded by seven mountain ranges and seven golden seas. Floating outside are the four world continents, each with a specific shape and orientation to a cardinal direction. Ours is the southern continent, Dzambuling, shown here at the left of the picture.*

tually powerful object or place is in one sense peculiarly Tibetan, having a firm foundation within their thoughts and actions. But in another sense it is a peculiarly human symbolic behavior, which is most predominant among those of the world's people still closely attuned to living in the natural world.

Lying just below the surface of the onion of Tibetan cosmology is a layer perhaps as old as the paleolithic. This view of the universe corresponds closely to the view contained in the spiritual practices of the Mongolians and Siberians. And this, in turn, closely parallels the way Native Americans of the Western hemisphere view their idealized universe.

For Tibetans, be they Buddhist monks or *bon-po* shamans, the cosmos consists of three circular planes impaled along a vertical tree-like axis. The world axis tree grows up through the center of the four sided cosmic mountain of the universe, *rirab lhungpo.* For

28

Buddhists the circularity is embodied in the wheel of the *dharma*; for shamans it is the circular drum upon which the consciousness travels throughout the cosmos, like a rider upon his horse.

The middle circle of the three symbolizes the earthly plane. It is populated by a variety of life forms: humans, animals, plants, and various noncorporeal beings. The latter include beings such as the hungry ghosts, which appear much like those said to haunt our own castles and homes; earth-bound environmental spirits living within the rocks, soil, trees and springs, which must be placated and pacified in order for humans to live harmoniously with the land; and potentially beneficial protector-deities of the environment.

Further up the vertical axis, backbone of the cosmos, floats the circle of sky realm. Here dwell gods and demigods living on the peaks of mountains and on lotus clouds.

The six realms of samsara, *or phenomenal existence, are illustrated in the following woodblock prints. At the core of Buddhist philosphy lies the concept of repeated rebirth of one's consciousness into one after the other of the six realms of sentient beings. Death and rebirth are inevitable until the consciousness eventually sees ordinary reality as illusion and suffering, and thereby breaks free from the endless cycle to attain enlightenment. Of the six realms, three are "fortunate" and three "unfortunate."*

29

Titans and gods (the two realms are combined into one picture). The titans, or demi-gods, are super-human in size and strength and have great wealth and power. Living within view of the gods they covet the gods' abode and blissful existence, and thus make war on them.

The gods live on lotus clouds at the top of the cosmic mountain, rirab lhungpo. They have no need of food or drink since they live off their own self-generated, inner light. They live in total bliss believing that they are immortal. However, they too are mortal and at the end of their long lives meet death entirely unprepared.

Humans. Human beings are most fortunate since they have the teachings of the Buddha. If they are prudent and wise, humans may prepare effectively for their rebirths and ultimate enlightenment by living compassionate and mindful lives and learning to understand the nature of reality.

Hungry ghosts. If sentient beings lead lives of acquisitiveness and greed, or if they become too attached to a person or thing, they may be reborn as a hungry ghost. Examples of such sentient beings are those that haunt houses. Hungry ghosts have huge bellies, pin sized mouths and skinny necks and are, therefore, unable to satisfy their constant hunger.

Hell beings. The Buddhist hell, like the Christian one, is a horrible place. The reborn consciousness of perpetrators of heinous deeds against other sentient beings are flailed, beaten, boiled, burned and frozen, among other fates. Unlike the Western hell, however, this one can be escaped, after one's accrued negative karma to experience such suffering has been expended.

31

Animals. While the realm of the animals is less dismal than those of the hungry ghosts and hell beings, it is still considered undesirable by Tibetans. Animals act primarily in an instinctual manner and must face a daily reality of searching for food and killing or being killed. As in the case of the other realms, someone who is born this lifetime as a human being can find themselves in the next life as an animal if he or she does not live life mindfully. Thus Tibetans, like all Buddhists, avoid killing animals. Indeed, they recognize the personal space and needs of non-visible beings as well, with whom humans and animals are said to coexist.

At the roots of the universal tree, countless miles below the great *stupa* at Bodh Gaya, lies the underworld realm. It is populated by tormented hell beings.

These three realms symbolically revolve around the "pillars of the sky, fixing pegs of the earth," as Tibetans call significant vertical sacred structures, sacred mountains, certain masonry pillars in temples, and special trees.

The vertical arrangement of the realms is also a metaphor for the levels of mind and action that fluctuate between better and worse in our paths through life. Taken as a whole they comprise the realms of *samsara*, the eternally revolving wheel of bondage to phenomenal existence and its attendant illusions and suffering. Among the realms, the eternal circle of life, death and rebirth continues until checked by the

His Holiness the Dalai Lama.

32

attainment of enlightenment.

One's lives thus move in cycles. They also move in a vertical, linear fashion, in the sense that the consciousness can develop or retrench throughout eternity, until it gains the necessary mental development to break free into the Buddha field.

The conception of an upward development of the consciousness in its yearning to burst the bonds of suffering is a universal metaphor. The comparison between cosmological realms and qualities of mind is shared by the Tibetans and their ancient brethren on both sides of the Pacific. The Tibetan scheme of the cosmos is repeated with slight variation by most native North Americans. The states of mind that Indians consider significant are equally symbolized in the three Tibetan levels of the gross, the subtle and the spirit.

The beings populating the three universal realms comprise for both Tibetans and their distant cousins in the New World, polytheistic pantheons that make up the totality or "oneness" of their respective universes. For Tibetans the pantheon consists of deities who are emanations of the total Buddha nature, plus the ambient consciousness of those beings not yet capable of bringing out the Buddha nature from within. For Native Americans naturally-occurring phenomena and life forms symbolize spiritual members of their pantheons. These function as convenient emblems of the components of their totality.

In both cases, the respective spiritual symbols serve as models for qualities of mind and action that are either to be emulated or avoided in order to achieve the ideal human consciousness. Systems so constituted have probably molded human development since the dawn of our species. And it is these very peoples, the Tibetans, American Indians and their soul mates worldwide living within the natural world, to whom we now turn for a direct infusion of basic human truths.

Offerings of blessing cords, mantras, prayer flags and tsa-tsa *line the circumambulation path. (Incense)*

Sang *incense billows from the roof of Namgyal Monastery in the early morning chill. (Incense)*

Wind Horses and Galloping Minds

Two of the most speedy and effective movers in human experience are the wind and the horse. One carries things lighter than our average weights, the other, things heavier.

For Tibetans the horse is also the bearer of thoughts. It is often likened to the mind. Milarepa, the beloved eleventh century yogi-hermit of Tibet, called the mind a galloping horse which, wishing to fly like the wind, must be harnessed to be useful.

The horse and wind merge for Tibetans into a sort of Pegasus which, like their other spiritual animals, may be seen only by those clarified enough to see them. They exist for the rest of us as a metaphor, to be experienced through belief.

Tibetans offer up prayers into the unseen spiritual world by means of another sort of wind horse. Tibetans call their prayer flag *lung ta*, literally meaning "wind horse." Each woodblock-printed flag carries prayers and invocations to deities, illustrations of auspicious animals: the wind horse, garuda bird, dragon, snow lion and tiger; and colors embodying the five basic elements: air, water, fire, earth and ether, or mind. They are imbued as well with the prayerful mental offerings of the people who make and use them. With each flutter in the wind, visible and invisible prayers are thus multiplied and sent off into the void for the benefit of those who made them and all other beings as well.

34

Lung ta, *the "wind horse." It symbolizes the swiftness and deliberateness with which the wind, as if it were a horse bearing a messenger on its saddle, carries the prayers of the people into the Buddha realm. Instead of a human rider it carries on its saddle a* norbu, *a flaming wish-fulfilling gem. Then one is said to have high* lung ta.

Accordingly, Tibetans refer to the state of their luck as having *lung ta:* "My *lung ta* is high today." *Lung tas* are strung up high on hills, from house top or tree to adjacent tree, and on vertical tree-branch poles marking the four cardinal directions at each corner of the roof of a house. They remain fluttering in the gales and bleaching in the rain and intense sunlight until they decompose away, in the process intimately melding their requests with the universal energy source beyond.

Lung tas on cloth flags and banners, *lung tas* in the wind, *lung tas* on paper scattered into the air from altars during *pujas, lung tas* in the material world and *lung tas* of the mind gallop along and help our spirits to fly.

In the wider sense, lung ta refers to the prayer flag of Tibet. It consists of woodblock-printed prayers, invocations and images of power-animals, on cloth. The customary power-animals are depicted at the corners and center of the flag. These are (clockwise from the upper left) cha kyung (garuda), the spiritual eagle devouring a snake; druk, the dragon, whose voice produces thunder, and flashing tongue, lightning; ta, the tiger, master of the forests; and seng ge, the snow lion, living in the glaciers of the Himalayas and the animal symbol of Tibet. In the center is the lung ta, the wind horse, which carries the prayers printed on the flag and in the minds of those who offer them, up into the Buddha realm with the speed of the wind and the horse. Like the prayers enclosed in the prayer wheel, when the prayer flags flutter in the breeze, their religious invocations are multiplied and sent off that many times on behalf of all sentient beings.

Light as Thoughts

Khatags (offering-scarves) are as light as thought and as transparent as air. Being exceedingly inexpensive, *khatags* are available to anyone who may wish to establish respectful contact between himself and another person or deity.

Khatags constitute offerings to the Dalai Lama and other revered lama reincarnates, to deities embodied in religious paintings, statues and shrines, to spirits in trees, and gods dwelling on mountain peaks. They are offered to all that are revered and to some that are feared. *Khatags* are placed around the neck of a traveller by friends who remain behind, the scarves bearing their well-wishes for a safe journey.

Khatags are thrown, tumbling and floating from one person ahead to the next, during teachings by the Dalai Lama, as if physical manifestations of their very thoughts. Like boiling clouds the scarves fill the air and collect before the throne in huge piles of white, which seem ready to take off at the slightest breeze. The individual grasps the *khatag* between his or her hands and after a meditative prayer tosses it up into the storm of white. In this way the offering of the single person is multiplied many times by all those who pass it on to the front, to lie at the feet of the revered lama.

Most *khatags* are simple pieces of open weave fabric. By their uniformity and simplicity they favor no individual as they link up the hearts and minds of

Offering gifts, including a khatag *scarf,* kapse *pastry, and money, to the* drekhar, *"white ghost," the masked bearer of good tidings at the new year.*

hundreds of people assembled within the view of the living Buddha.

Khatags can be wind horses. Like the printed prayer flags they are offered into the wind and the void beyond from atop banners, flag poles, and among strings of prayer flags strung from rooftops to wind-gnarled trees.

Khatags on the neck of pilgrims are offered to the Dalai Lama as he gives his blessings during the New Year observances. Those blessed derive, in turn, a tiny bit of his power, which now is infused within the *khatag's* weblike weave.

By physical standards *khatags* are flimsy, loosely woven scarves of cotton or, less frequently, silk. Their physical qualities, therefore, do not reveal their weightiness. Nor can it be measured by any meter or scale. *Khatags* weigh heavily only on the balance of belief that measures the power generated by a person's hopes, prayers and good wishes. It is as if their very flimsiness of form and openness of weave allow room for these intangible portions of mental power to be contained within. Like the wind, like the events of the mind, the *khatag* seems almost not to exist. This tenuous nature, verging on non-existence, makes the *khatag* a perfect medium for sending greetings into the realm of the spirit.

Part II Living in the World

Snow

Tibetans refer to their country as *Khawachen*, "Land of Snows." Snow caps the mountains the year round. It blankets the lower-lying countryside with a mantle of white for but a brief while, only to sublimate directly into water vapor in the intense sunlight, disappearing before one's very eyes.

Snow melts into mountain run-off. It fuels mighty rivers coursing through profound canyons and irrigates thirsty fields of barley and wheat. At the same moment that a portion returns to liquid, newer snowfall becomes transformed into monstrous glaciers whose leading edges ultimately return to water, perhaps ten thousand years after first having fallen.

Glaciers are the realm of the legendary white snow lions with turquoise manes, the symbols of Tibet. The Tibetans, likewise, are lions of the snow but with turquoise around their necks, on their fingers, and in their ears.

While a Tibetan will never deprecate a balmy day, with a good snowstorm here in Dharamsala, work is set aside for many a nostalgic look around and a wild snowball free-for-all.

In the West, snowball fights are reserved mainly for children and only rarely participated in by adults. This is understandable since parents and their peers lose their sense of humor, for the most part, as they gain in years: "Oh, Johnny, you'll catch a cold out there; oh well, boys will be boys; anyway, he'll soon grow out of it."

The seng ge, snow lion, *is the mythological animal-dweller of the high glaciers. It has been described as approximately one meter in length, white with turquoise colored mane and tail, and having the uncanny ability to jump from one mountain peak to the next. It is said that the* seng ge *can bounce off one peak and return to the next without ever touching down. The snow lion is the customary animal symbol of Tibet; a pair (male and female) adorn the national flag.*

40

But not here. In fact, despite initial efforts to the contrary (having been conditioned by those warnings during my childhood), I have become brainwashed by the Tibetan *laissez-faire* in living and have lost all inhibition to a good snowball fight. The sight of middle-aged Tibetan matrons, in traditional dress as old as Asia itself, cavorting in the company of a band of army-coated, long-haired young Tibetan men while they ambushed passersby with huge snowballs, was the final straw. Those venerable *ama-las* ("mothers" as they are respectfully addressed by younger Tibetans) immediately infected me with their exuberant smiles. And it didn't take long for the initial shock to wear off, all the more hastened by a huge clump of snow down the back of my neck, neatly pitched by an hysterically laughing Tibetan grandmother.

So what could I do? Be the objective observer? Hell no. I hit her back with a snowball, and she laughed even harder. Now things were getting serious. Grandmas were pelting grandchildren. Young bucks a hundred feet down the road by the Tibetan Medical Centre were lobbing long-range bombs at the *ama-las*. And everyone was smashing at the poor Indians, returning from a pilgrimage to a Shiva shrine farther down the road.

And that was funny to watch. The faster they ran the more they got pelted. But in all fairness, many did fight back admirably and soon there ensued a free-for-all that was as remarkable for the amount of laughter as for the volume of white stuff flying through the air.

Of Birds and Buddhists

A Westerner here in Dharamsala observed the other day that "Buddhist places always seem to attract birds." I thought that comment over for a while. I reflected back to my days in New Delhi and the many birds I had seen there. Hindus, too, were quite respectful of birds of every kind, holding, as they do, to non-violence. And certainly in the cities there was enough organic waste scattered around for the birds to feast upon.

But up here in the mountains there is less refuse and fewer rodent scavengers for the sharp-eyed airborne predators to score. And I was equally struck by the absence of birds just down the road at the Indian village, despite its terraced gardens, cows, sheep, goats and chickens, seemingly a good environment for birds to thrive on.

Yet, birds are everywhere here in the Tibetan neighborhood of McLeod Ganj. Little sparrow types clean up the small morsels of bread or flour left behind by careless two-legged creatures.

The in-close, ground-to-air scene, however, is dominated by big, bluish-black ravens. Traveling in packs, they caw and grunt continuously to each other. Engrossed in their games, they nevertheless have a keen eye on the lookout for a fast meal.

Ravens are the jokers of the local bird society; they always seem to be having fun. Yesterday was a case in point. The wind was almost up to gale force and it seemed to excite the ravens even more than would a calm day on which they would languishingly ride the thermals down the mountainside. As if taking part in a well-structured children's schoolyard game, they dove in turn, from pine and rhododendron trees, off the ridge into the turbulent air. Captured immediately by a ferocious gust, each *kamikaze* raven would be transported immediately out of view.

Recovering from what seemed suicidal leaps, some miraculously maneuvered to other tree branches, their wings bent into almost impossible shapes, aerodynamic in only the most bizarre of air flows. Even more astoundingly, many skillfully settled to earth ever so gently, slender feet fully extended, stretching toward solid ground.

When you consider the delicacy of the parts with which birds' wings are assembled you can appreciate my trepidation and amazement at the contortions that those birds' wings underwent in the service of a good time.

And it became all the more apparent that despite being "lesser" members of the animal kingdom, these birds had full-fledged, integrated consciousnesses and were not simply eating, flying and mating machines. No doubt countless Tibetans have meditated on this point through the ages.

Other birds took their work more seriously. Vultures have always been enigmas to me. They are studies in duality. You see them busy at work on roadside carrion and when you come closer they leap into flight as if furtive burglars caught in the act.

As ugly as a vulture is up close, it is one of the most remarkably beautiful birds when in flight. Its luxurious wings are surely like those that Icarus chose for his daring flight into the sun.

And like the naked Icarus the vulture too lacks plumage, but only about the head, giving it an ugly, scar-like countenance. These characteristics, in addition to its ecologically sound yet, for some, distasteful role of carrion eater, gives the vulture its checkered reputation. Tibetans, like other nature-people, seem to be able to sort these out and turn this duality into a certain appreciation.

The vulture has served Tibetans faithfully at the most crucial time in their phenomenal existence, death. Tibetans believe that the corpse is an empty shell, formerly the shelter and physical manifestor of the deceased's now wandering consciousness. For up to forty-nine days after death it seeks its rebirth. The body, in the meantime, must be rejoined to the four basic elements out of which it was originally constituted.

There were four options in old Tibet: return to the fire-element through cremation; return to the water-element by giving it to the rivers; return to the earth-element through burial; and return to the air-element. The latter was done by carefully dismembering the body at a special charnel ground. The flesh was cut up into small pieces and the bone powdered into meal and mixed with brain, all for the pleasure of the carrion birds, vultures reigning supreme.

But, to my mind, the greatest symbols of the sky realm are the hawks and eagles that fly all about these mountain crags and evergreen forests. The kites, a form of hawk, grace us with their diving, swooping flight and click-click, twisting, darting heads and eyes. Spiraling upwards on the thermal convections of air, they carry our thoughts up to the imaginary line of airy height that they dare to share with the eagles.

Eagles populate the highest reaches of the sky. They ride the thermals, spiraling, seemingly without effort, up the mountainsides, then back down gracefully into the valley several thousand feet below. Stiff wings stretch out from their bodies. Fingertip-like flight feathers project out from wingtips into space, licking the air, making minute adjustments, compensating for wind eccentricities too subtle for heavy creatures such as ourselves to ever imagine.

The eagles spiral upward, bringing our thoughts and sight with them into the domain of the snow lion. To Tibetans the eagles are the masters of the highest rocky crags that punctuate the glacial fields, while snow lions represent the glaciers.

Tibetans also have their spiritual eagle, the *cha kyung*. Like the Native American Thunderbird, it embodies the spiritual power of the sky. Originating in the dim haze of ancient Asian beliefs, the *cha kyung* is depicted devouring its enemy, a snake. Later, when Buddhism came to Tibet, along came the eagle-like *garuda* bird, a similar spiritual creature based in Hindu mythology. Knowing eagles as dwellers of the highest realm along the cosmological world-axis linking the underworld, earth's surface, and sky, Tibetans readily fit the *garuda* into their spiritual landscape.

The world of the bird is the kind of world Tibetans understand. Perhaps that's why birds like the Buddhists.

The cha kyung *is the spiritual monarch of the sky realm. A mythological animal from ancient Asian folk belief, it fits well into the Tibetan view of the spiritual universe. When Buddhism arrived in Tibet 1300 years ago, it brought with it elements of the earlier Hindu religion. These included the mythological* garuda *bird. Tibetans syncretized the two and today use both names interchangeably.*

45

Chang

Every culture has its national drink. And in my travels, I have eagerly sipped as many such beverages as I could possibly find. This vast body of experience has led me to conclude that each drink enhances a certain quality of the consciousness of its users.

Some drinks are boisterous, some contemplative. Some heavy, some light. Some darken the mind while others lighten the way. Some allow you to retain control, others relieve you of it.

Not all humans drink distilled beverages, but all seem to have beer. I have had beer that was as tasteless as the people who prided themselves on drinking it; beer that was as heavy in flavor and alcohol as the jocks who swigged it; and beer as weak as the fear of it in those who watered it. But until I had spent time with Tibetans, I had never had a beer that took me to such unexplored mental heights.

The name of this secret brew is *chang*. Originally fermented from barley, the subsistence grain of high altitude Tibet, it is also likely to get you higher than any other beer would. Here in India it is made from whatever grain is close at hand, namely wheat, rice or millet.

Chang is a milky, beige-colored drink made through the simple fermentation of wheat kernels. The boiled mass — corresponding to our corn mash — is left to ferment in the presence of yeast. I suspect that its very simplicity of manufacture, combined with the altitude at which it is drunk, and definitely the company with whom it is shared, contributes to its incisive, almost psychedelically clarifying properties. And I can say with certainty that — except for the times I have taken certain naturally-occurring psychedelics and the national drinks of Scandinavia and Mexico, aquavit and tequila — I never see the world so clearly as when I am drinking *chang*.

Here is Migmar's recipe for making *chang*. She brewed this batch up for a birthday party I recently attended:

Migmar's Chang

1. Boil 17 kilos of wheat for 1½ hours, as for rice. After it soaks up water let it sit for 3 hours in the pot.

2. After 3 hours lay out the wet wheat on a slab or table. Let it cool until it is about room temperature on a pleasant day (less than lukewarm).

Guests visiting a household at the New Year take a customary pinch of chemar *and a drop of* chang *beer. They flick these into the air with the exclamation "tashi delek!" ("good luck!") The hosts then proceed to urge each guest to drink no less than three bowls of* chang.

3. Put 17 tabs of *chang* yeast (1 tab, approximately 2 heaped tablespoons) into bowl. Add some flour; crush; then spread it evenly among the wheat.

4. Put this into a pot; put some live coals and roasted barley flour in the center in a ritualistic manner.

5. Put pot in a pleasant dark place — not too warm/ not too cold.

6. Cover wheat with paper and several layers of burlap and canvas — 3 layers on top and bottom for early spring — more or less for winter or summer.

7. After 3 days of fermentation you can transfer wheat mash to sealed tins or jars.

8. Use: morning before evening use — 2 parts wheat to 3 parts water or if wheat is strong, 2 to 4.

This recipe is for "women's *chang*." For "men's *chang*" ferment 3 or 4 days or longer, up to one year.

Chang is drunk all year round but is most appreciated during *losar*, the New Year's season, and on festive occasions such as weddings. Many households brew their own. Others hire beaming, exquisitely wrinkled, chocolate-skinned, ivory-toothed *ama-las* to do it for them.

At *losar* time *chang* serves several functions. It firmly transports the user into the appropriately festive state of mind. As a social offering it conveys the hospitable well wishes of the household when it is visited by friends, relatives and neighbours. It is one of the standard ritual offerings to the deities, being placed on altars for the purpose, or into the sacred smoky fire during *pujas*.

When one is offered *chang* one does not refuse, nor indeed can refuse, a glass or three or more. I learned this the hard way on the second day of *losar*. That day, as did many hundreds of others in Dharamsala, my friend Dale and I went off visiting Tibetan friends.

Tibetan grandmothers pray and prostrate before the statue of the Buddha, sitting within the temple doors. (The Golden Buddha by the Sacred Juniper)

An ancient juniper tree and banks of prayer wheels, at the northwest corner of the temple. (The Golden Buddha by the Sacred Juniper)

The devout and admiring welcome the Dalai Lama back to the town with prayers and smoking incense sticks. (Sunbeams in the Drizzle)

The day began with blessings by the Dalai Lama. In full Tibetan dress, fresh from the blessings, Dale and I paid our first New Year's visit to Ama-la and Kalsang, proprietors of the former popular breakfast spot, the Last Chance Tea Shop.

"Last Chance *Ama-la*" is a memorable character. She would lean over the low kerosene stove cooking eggs "just as you like 'em," singing and dancing in her seat while joking with her motley crew of Euro-American customers. A diplomatic and genuinely happy soul is she, and today Last Chance *Ama-la* was in rare form.

We entered her shop, and after we had been offered pieces of *kapse*, the traditional *losar* pastry, *Ama-la* ambled over to our table with what looked like a recycled Johnny Walker bottle, filled with that telltale creamy-beige liquid.

The bottle's neck was wrapped with a piece of gauzey cotton *khatag*. I had been seeing decorations such as this everywhere during *losar*; around water spigots, faucets, reservoirs of various kinds, and at pools formed by the natural seepage of springs. One young Tibetan woman explained that as water was the source of life, they must show respect for it. Certainly the offering of the *khatag* is one of the primary signs of respect.

What better time to renew one's social or spiritual contract than during this time of yearly renewal. The fact that such *khatag* offerings (along with three pats of butter and occasional *torma* sculptures) are given to the water, suggests that Tibetans are recognizing the power of the *lü*, the natural spirit dwellers of the watery world. They are mischievous; indeed, some are potentially harmful. To neglect their desires, not to mention their existence, could be the source of great misfortune; to show them respect through offerings is that necessary ounce of prevention. Likewise, when the Last Chance *Ama-la* offered us the *chang* from her

Khatag *scarves hang from a plaque at the shrine to* Palden Lhamo, *the fierce protectress of the Tibetan people. (Light As Thoughts)*

Snow comes in on wings of powerful storms and blankets Dharamsala with a luxurious mantle of white. (Snow)

khatag-collared bottle she offered up to her guests a message of respect.

Ama-la filled our glasses to the brim. Floating in it were kernels of wheat. Residue of imperfect straining, they were also symbols of the Tibetan closeness to the natural way of doing things.

"Drink up boys!" was *Ama-la*'s implied message as she hovered over us, bottle in hand, after having poured us our first *chang*. Circumstances such as this sometimes give rise to uneasy emotions. One is, after all, accepting another's hospitality, yet one also wishes that she would withdraw the subtle pressure of over-eager hospitality. Then I remembered having been told about being expected to accept three fillings of the *chang* glass on first entering someone's home. Hearty souls down the glass before each refilling. The more conservative (and quite the wiser) take a mouthful or two and then extend the glass twice for refilling to the brim.

This latter approach is more a matter of theory than practice. That old devil *chang* seems to have a way of seducing you into gulping down three full glasses. Perhaps this is because only the very strongest *chang* contains even the slightest hint of that acrid alcoholic principle. *Chang* is smooth, light and sweet in flavor, mildly reminiscent of a vanilla milkshake. All-in-all, *chang* is a most pleasant drink, the more so it seemed after four glasses of *Ama-la*'s home brew.

Staggering into the morning sunshine, the next uncertain step was to attend a *losar* "tea" party at the quarters of the owners of our residence. I was a little surprised at the indirect description of the party, considering that these folks had been making *chang* for days during the weeks previous to *losar*.

The hotel *ama-la*, a handsome and outspoken woman, made it most clear to me during the previous week that I and my Tibetan banjo-lute, the *damnyen*, were both cordially invited to attend.

50

I am generally shy about giving command performances, especially on an instrument that I had been studying for scarcely one month. But I also knew that the old faithful *chang* would effectively reduce my inhibitions and clarify my concentration to an exceptional degree. True to prediction, all went well. Tibetans love music, and they love foreigners who play their music.

The strings plucked; the songs swelled; the *chang* flowed; and, at last, Peter staggered up to his room, the *chang*-induced coda reaching what could only be described as its final crescendo, in his head.

It was now six-thirty p.m. and Dale, Marcia and I were about to embark on the hike up the mountain to the Tibetan Music, Dance and Drama Society (now the Tibetan Institute of Performing Arts). There was a party planned for the evening. The students and staff at the Drama Society had been planning it for weeks and the *chang* they had been brewing promised to be most tasty.

It was approaching dark by the time three hungover, slightly inebriated *Injis* (Westerners) commenced our climb up the hillside below the Drama Society. We decided on the rocky approach rather than the road, not out of suicidal inclination, but in order to deliver our New Year's cards to Lama Yeshe Dorje, a tantric master who lived halfway up the ridge. Yeshe Dorje was one of the friendliest and jolliest men around, and we had taken an immediate liking to him.

After much unsteady climbing we arrived at his *gompa*, a temple attached to his modest house. We entered the *gompa* to be greeted by two of his assisting monks, one of whom Marcia had affectionately dubbed "the laughing monk." They greeted us warmly, laughing.

Laughing Monk led us to the altar. There we each took a pinch of *tsamba* from the offering box and cast it three times over our right shoulders repeating "*tashi*

delek'' (''good luck'') with each throw, a common New Year's custom. On taking our seats Laughing Monk continued the hospitality from out of a two-gallon jerry-can filled with, you guessed it, *chang*.

Like their lay brothers and sisters, their hospitality abounded, as did the *chang*. By the end of a three- or four- glass session (things had begun to blur when it came to counting) we were ready to float up the hill, vaguely in the direction of the Drama Society. I was so far gone by this point that I had left my hat, shoulder bag and a dozen oranges and apples at the *gompa*, forgetting for days afterward even where they were!

Bidding our laughing and mischievous holy hosts good-bye, we continued our rubbery climb.

By the time we succeeded in arriving at the Drama Society, the party was already in progress, although just barely. Despite the spontaneous and open qualities of the Tibetans, especially these young performer

Large bowls of chang *help fuel the* gorshey, *ancient round dances, done on festive occasions such as weddings and the New Year.*

types, the party was not what one would call particularly lively. We soon discovered that it would be up to us to inject some life into the proceedings.

Within minutes of our arriving, out came the *chang*. It was served up in big aluminum kettles usually reserved for supplying the massive tea breaks held several times daily during classes and practice sessions. And the tradition of downing three containers full of *chang* was strictly adhered to here, but with one characteristic embellishment.

One's hosts, *chang* in hand, would stand around awaiting the refill request, singing a traditional *chang* drinking song. Thus one is serenaded until having completed the required three rounds of *chang*. This is pressure at its subtlest. At first the singing is a flattering touch; having the ears as well as the palate catered to is a most pleasurable experience. But before long the pleasant songs become hints to the guest to hurry up and get on with the serious business of

Members of the Tibetan Institute of Performing Arts (formerly Music, Dance and Drama Society) perform and preserve the beautiful old dances and operatic dramas of Tibet.

drinking. The guest tries to draw the drinking out as long as possible so as not to shock the system too severely, but the hosts have, after all, many more mouths to fill. The guest, while loving the song, does not wish to make the hosts stand there all night singing, so rapidly down goes the *chang*. All that would come to mind during those moments was the popular refrain, "Killing Me Softly With His Song."

This was a special night for me. Certainly because I'd lost by this time all inhibitions (not to mention gross motor coordination), but especially because I was finally going to have my chance to perform my own music for these, the cream of Tibetan performing artists.

A few of the musicians had heard me play Appalachian mountain tunes on the *damnyen*; "Shady Grove," "The Cuckoo," and "Across the Rocky Mountains" were naturals on it. Tibetan and American mountain music are extremely close in sound, and the *damnyen* is quite reminiscent of a fretless banjo. In addition, tonight I was to play a number of American mountain tunes, and even a few Russian ones, on a five-string banjo that Dale and I had hurriedly built over the previous three days from tambourine, *sitar* and umbrella parts!

The Tibetans seemed to enjoy it. I know I did. The *chang* no doubt helped. So the evening progressed, and equally did our states of intoxication. But *chang* clarifies as well as numbs and as long as my fingers retained their senses I kept taking my turn at the microphone.

The evening developed into a hootenanny for tipsy Tibetans and rubbery Westerners. Poems, Tibetan opera passages and folk songs, Hindi film tunes, Appalachian banjo and Russian *balalaika* tunes, even Everly Brothers' ballads, were amplified indoors. What we didn't know at the time was that it was also broadcast over the P.A. down the mountainside to town!

After the initial shock of self-consciousness had worn off, the thought of my vocal indecent exposure in public really didn't seem to matter. After all, the entire town was by this time in a liquid-wheat-induced state closely paralleling our own.

Tashi delek, punsumtsok, Happy New Year!

Green (and Red and White and Yellow and Blue) Is the Color

Tibetans revel in a kaleidoscope of color. Colors flash from prayer flags, float off women's aprons and glint from jewels around their necks. They dart frenetically from children's woolen pantaloons, glow from silk-framed religious paintings, billow from maroon robes of monks strolling alone against the white of distant mountains, and shine from golden temple roofs.

Red, blue, yellow, white and green vibrate helter-skelter into a riot of rainbow colors. Red of rhododendron blossoms and coral stones, blue of water and sky, yellow of the sun, green of the trees, and white of the snow compose the rainbow world in which Tibetans pass their lives.

Beings living in the unseen realm of the universe also bask in the rainbow's colors. *Khadomas*, sky-going celestial fairies, ethereal creatures of the Buddha realm and messengers of the deities, sport elegant headdresses of rainbow colors. They carry saints to heavenly places along rainbow bridges. A tantric master receives the energy and mind of an invoked deity along a rainbow cord — twisted strands of the five colors placed against his heart.

Yellow signifies earth; red, fire; green, water; blue, sky; and white, ether, or mind. Prayer flags of these five colors link house or tree to other trees, making the town look as if it were captured in an intricate but haphazard spider's web of rainbows.

All are pure colors, direct, primary colors; all except green. Green, the unity of yellow and blue, gives the mind a respite from the primal eruptions of the other four. Restful and conciliatory, the color green is also the personal birth color of the present Dalai Lama, who himself evokes the qualities of conciliation and calm of mind.

Green is the favored color for flags and banners. They are edged in red or yellow to emphasize the greenness. Hanging out a green flag reinforces the devoutness of the householder and amplifies the power and importance of the Dalai Lama.

My residence, the Phande Green House, is painted green. The woodwork and walls, the restaurant, even the pillars on which the name is painted, are green.

The turquoise mane and tail of the Snow Lion, animal emblem of Tibet, are green.

Green is the color of one form of *Tara*, the wish-fulfilling Buddha. She is the Tibetan symbol of boundless fertility, the Great Goddess.

A Tibetan friend expresses her love for green in the interior decor of her room. The wooden table, tablecloth, louvers above window and door, are all painted green. Her sweater is green. "I love green," says she.

Once I had the pleasure of speaking with Ngari Rinpoche, youngest brother of the Dalai Lama. I asked him what green meant to him, in light of it being the birth color of the Dalai Lama. He responded that, to him, green signified a spiritual flourishing: "Like the book, *The Greening of America*, I feel there is a greening of the spirit that the world is slowly experiencing. This is what green means to me."

A Walk into the Himalayas

McLeod Ganj sits cradled atop a Himalayan foothill ridge that juts proudly out over the rolling Kangra Valley of northern India. On the highest immediate point sits the palace of the Dalai Lama, and slightly below it, the main temple of the Tibetans in exile.

The double camel-hump of rock, soil, water and trees is a fingertip of the most massive mountain range on earth. The Himalayas are alive in their inexorable tectonic movement — young by geological time, but more ancient than even the reckonings of the ancient Tibetans, children of its snows.

McLeod Ganj sits low within the Himalayan continuum, only 6,000 feet above the sea, yet one has the definite impression of being in the middle of mountains. Snow and hail impact mercilessly on pine- and rhododendron-covered slopes, and most of the year the rocky massifs looming above bear a mantle of freshly-fallen snow.

Fog and rain are carried in on wings of ferocious winds. Rays of sunlight ever come and go. Fluctuating light and dark, damp and dry, cold and warm, the razor-clear procession of the stars, moon and sun are mountain traits that remind the Tibetans (as all mountain lovers) of home.

While Tibetans in exile now look toward the world below for economic and political support, for their spiritual sustenance they look to the Dalai Lama and beyond into the snow mountains gesturing compellingly from above the trees.

Mountains are the dwelling places and, symbolically, the embodiments of the *yullha*, gods of the environment. They are the anchoring points upon which Tibetans moor their cosmological landscape of the sky, earth, underworld, and cardinal directions. Mountains are referred to as "pillars of the sky, fixing pegs of the earth," for they are clear and ever-present reminders of the universal centrality that we call the *axis mundi*. Likewise, they serve the Tibetans as convenient reminders of the need for centering the activities of body and mind here and now.

It is not surprising that Tibetans manifest this centrality of mind, body and environment by means of surrogate rocky cairns. These loosely-piled rocky markers, found at mountain passes or in view of sacred spots such as the approaches to the palace of the Dalai Lama, are mortared by prayers and sculpted by cries of *lha gyal lo!* (victory to the gods!). In placing small rocks atop the cairns, Tibetans center themselves inwardly as solidly as in the rock of the mountains centered into the earth.

Sensing this mountain metaphor ever more strongly as the weeks went by, I increasingly felt the need to climb up closer to these powerful vertical expressions of the earth's power.

I had no desire to experience the snow mountains in a *macho*, because-it's-there manner, but wished only to allow my senses to open, to clear the channels of my heart and mind. I felt that opening up in a profound encounter with alpine power would be personally healing, and at the same time give me considerably more insight into the Tibetan view of things.

The day came in late April when the trail to Triund, the apex of the local foothills, was finally passable. Marcia, the anthropologist, Kenji, the Japanese Zen Buddhist *thangka* painter, and I decided on an early start. It is a three-and-a-half-hour trek to Triund, and in spring the weather would not allow a full day of clear and calm. We had to reach Triund, therefore, well before early afternoon in order to catch a full frontal glimpse of the snow range before the sharp crags snagged an impenetrable veil of clouds.

And so it began. And here was the first hill to climb. Up we went past the small wooden houses of former Tibetan country folk. Their houses were built closely shadowing the ridge sides, at times more ridge than house. Some of the walls consisted more of living tree than the wooden slats of dead ones. Large trees, gnarled by the ceaseless wind, stood cockeyed in among the houses. For Tibetans, these trees sheltered not only birds but earth spirits. Since one must not tamper with the dwellings of spirits, the trees were left to stand. It seems to me that these simple shacks represent the best in the wisdom of earthly living.

As we got part way up the ridge we encountered several spiritually significant objects. Scattered about were multicolored thread crosses, known as *namkha*. Translated somewhat romantically into English as "spirit catchers," these crosses, made from concentric windings of colored threads onto variously shaped geometric wooden frames, served to attract unwanted spirit entities away from a person or place.

The *namkha* is commonly used to entice malevolent spirits from an ill person's body. Tibetans believe that, in addition to somatic illnesses, there are illnesses caused by spirit possession. The lamas and astrologers divine which cause it is, and the patients seek out the appropriate aid. If the cause is a spirit, a disease-curing *puja* is prescribed whereby the offending agent is banished from the body. When the distasteful work is done, the *namkhas*, ritual arrows fleched in the five sacred colors, sculpted butter and barley *tormas*, thin sticks covered with written *mantras*, and scattered Indian coins, remain as bizarre and intriguing evidence of spiritual surgery. These anti-offerings are often rudely discarded over a hillside, and this particular hillside seemed to be the one most commonly chosen.

Up we pursued, past the Drama Society and its commanding view of the Kangra Valley. We arrived at the former grounds of a British colonial family, now a curious mixture of residences for respected lamas, nomadic Commonwealth hippies, and Kenji, our Zen Buddhist artist friend. Kenji was the perfect companion for this sort of trek, being sensitively attuned to the power of the natural world.

As we snaked up the mountainside, the Indian villages below began to fade into the cultivated terraces surrounding them.

Up we hiked, past a Hindu shrine to the goddess *Kali*. Curiously, it is perched on a rather arid, hilly spot as are so many other Hindu temples and villages in the vicinity. Trees do not seem to be common features in Indian settlements, at least in this area. Indians seem to always walk amidst bright, dry light, mirrored in parched earth tones. Tibetans, on the other hand, seem to blend into the flower- and foliage-covered mountainsides.

The real trek began as we passed the *Kali* shrine and embarked upon a winding stony path up the adjacent mountainside. Here we fully encountered springtime in the Himalayas, and its hallmark — the intense red spectrum of rhododendrons in bloom. Patches of fluorescent crimson and pink spotlit deep green leaves and gray rock. No small bushes these rhododendrons, but full-grown trees, some rivaling in breadth all but the older trees of the deciduous forests back home.

Water cascaded down shadowy folds of igneous flesh. They became, at higher altitudes, temporary glaciers hiding dripping ice caves within their folds.

Delicate wild flowers peeked out from rocky clefts and filigrees of ferns. The heady, sometimes overwhelming aroma of last year's leaves mixed with this year's rhododendron blossoms suffocated in an exquisite olfactory way. Up and up we climbed, yet the sun stayed ever hot as altitude compensated little for the swelter of the rising lowland heat.

The huge triangular snow mountain — whose name I never seemed to have had the need to discover — beckoned more intensely now; my eyes felt its rocky skin more fully.

We were going to have a good trudge through snow. At its latitude, Dharamsala doesn't experience the white stuff frequently enough for my taste. Despite being fifty miles from Tibet as the crow flies, I began to feel now for the first time the physical sensation of truly being in Tibet.

Triund began to loom accessibly above us. Its treeless saddle ridgeback, with its commanding view of Dharamsala and the Kangra Valley farther below, looked refreshingly cool and clean. As we attained its level, walking atop its subtly domed spine, the stretch of snow mountains rapidly loomed up; they snapped into sudden existence with all their intensity and power.

This, indeed, was Tibet. This was the first main ridge of Himalayan snow mountains, small in comparison with those sheltering Tibetans back home, but especially powerful since they represented the leading edge of the Indo-Asian tectonic uplift that Tibetans call *khawachen*, Land of Snows.

There is something about being among snow mountains that liberates. Instead of dwarfing the spirit, they inspire. They suggest solid centeredness on the one hand and infinite reach on the other.

The clouds up here were no longer ambiguous. They moved by rocky crags with measurable speed. They hovered between one's eyes and the mountains above and beyond, corralled like cattle in the lap of these monstrous earthworks.

The clouds moved in and out, suspended as if by magic within incredible rocky canyons. At first they hid, then revealed, the massive peaks. It occurred to me that the now-you-see-me-now-you-don't games minds play in environments such as this surely must serve as powerful lessons regarding illusion and impermanence to the Tibetans. In fact, it would seem that their pragmatic awareness of the natural world allowed them to develop ideas about the great voidness of things well before the first Indian Buddhist teachers arrived, carrying similar concepts developed through years of intense meditative thought.

The scorpion is a fiercesome animal both in its natural state and as a form taken by lü, *spirits of the watery world. Woodblock prints of scorpions are used as charms to ward off attack by harmful spirit entities. This type of charm is generally used to protect against four kinds of negative beings:* gyalpo, *demons;* dremo, *female ghosts;* sadag, *masters of the earth; and* lü.

Part III Portraits

At a Teaching by the Dalai Lama

By northern European standards I am experiencing a difficult problem. I am being crushed amid a mass of people as I sit here uncomfortably straddling the edge of a damp earthen incline. I listen along with thousands of others to the man they call His Holiness give a discourse on a subject about which I can barely catch the meaning of isolated phrases. That its implications are powerful needs no translation. The words capture the hearts and minds and, it would seem, the very breaths of those gathered here.

Had I been in a crowd this large and congested back home my paranoia would already have been bounding along at full speed. I would have been concentrating as much on the security of my camera and tape recorder as on the object of the gathering. I would be assailed by coughs and grunts and what would seem to be sickeningly sweet and sour personal odors. I would feel much more conscious of my personal image than I do here, despite the obvious fact that I am a white poppy among the red, a Caucasian among mountain Asiatics.

Yet such thoughts barely seem to matter at this moment. I don't seem to mind the young woman's knee grinding into my back, nor the child dribbling candy juice onto my shoulder.

I am feeling quite intimate with the devout middle-aged man, emanating the musky worn aroma of the years, sitting American-Indian-style before me. His unruly European-style haircut can't quite cover the ghost of a long braid that was·wrapped around the crown of his head with gaily-colored yarn in earlier days.

I don't seem to mind the *pugutso*, the lovely, curious little Tibetan children who at this moment watch me with great interest and in rapt attention as I write this essay in my little spiral notebook. An event strange enough here in the Himalayas, it is made even more curious to them by my use of the left hand for the purpose.

Nor do I mind the young boy leaning on my left wrist, making writing even more of a task. All the while he cracks peanuts between his teeth leaving little presents of pulverized shell on my pages.

And I certainly do not mind the young nomad type, mocha-skinned, clad in a black homespun woolen *chuba* cloak. His ears are pierced with turquoise. Pinch me, am I dreaming, or is this Arizona and isn't he a Navajo? Funny, but isn't the Tibetan slang word for hillbilly, *abaho*, amazingly appropriate? Who knows whether, having come from some far and out-of-the-way place, he perfectly understands the educated dialect of the Dalai Lama? Certainly his eyes and riveted attention suggest he does.

I like being near the old *ama-la* with round, immensely powerful tortoise-shell eyeglasses. She ardently fingers her crystal rosary beads and invokes her deity through *mantra* with the surety of long years of devotion.

I enjoy being around the young men and women who are Tibetan government workers, carpet weavers, teachers and traders. They proudly wear their best *chubas* and jewelry. For the moment, at least, they seem to be able to cast away their everyday concerns and partake in this communal meeting of hearts and minds.

I do like being around the corpulent *ama-la* who has

brought her *apso* dog, as if a child or treasured friend, to be blessed by His Holiness's words and presence.

And I certainly like being around the monks and nuns whose equanimity of action and mellowness of facial geography remind me of how I would like to fare in times of personal storm.

All these actors and scenery are bathed in the filigree of the warmly percussive voice of the Dalai Lama. His speech penetrates the crowd gently but firmly, like a clean breeze through a glade of springtime grass.

The Weatherman, Weather or Not

It's raining and storming this evening. Here in my
little room, snug with the heat of a kerosene stove and
writing in pioneer spirit by candle light, thoughts appropriately turn to Lama Yeshe Dorje, the Dalai Lama's
official weatherman.

In the West, weathermen provide advance warning
to a populace afraid of the slightest sprinkling and
terrified of storms. But here, among hearty people of
the snowline, in a land of intense extremes of drought,
rain, hail, wind and snow, the weatherman is much
more than a flaccid media personality telling you which
way the wind is blowing.

Yeshe Dorje is more popularly known by two other
titles, *Ngagpa-la* and Rainmaker. *Ngagpas* are the spirit
technicians of Tibetan society. They are trained to recognize and exert control over the invisible forces that
operate around their communities. As such, Yeshe
Dorje and fellow members of his exceptional profession
provide the service of interlocution between the people
and those members of the spirit realm who have control over natural phenomena.

One of his essential roles in old Tibet was that
of providing rain during untenable dry periods. In
Tibet, cultivation of high altitude crops such as barley
and wheat is a precarious affair requiring irrigation
systems supplied by mountain run-off. At these high
altitudes the air is very dry, the mountainous heights
having precipitated any moisture carried up from the

lowlands well before it might reach into the sheltered river valleys. Accordingly, Yeshe Dorje and his fellow *ngagpas* provide the techno-spiritual service of coaxing rain from the clouds.

More often than not his primary role continues to be that of rainstopper. The structure of the Himalayan range, which prevents moisture from directly watering the fields, can also create the most sudden and violent downpours.

The druk, *or dragon, is one of the five major spiritual power-animals of Tibet. It inhabits the storm clouds. Tibetans say that when a storm is in progress one can see the* druks *in action in the boiling, churning mass of grey moisture. They also tell us that thunder is the voice of the dragon, while lightning is its flicking tongue.*

The Himalayas are a series of awesome rocky ridges at times jutting up into the jet stream itself. Formed by the cutting action of glaciers and rivers, the successive canyons serve as natural wind tunnels. When moisture-laden air does venture into these inner recesses, it may undergo a violent metamorphosis producing intense lightning, thunder, rain, wind and, very commonly, hail.

70

Hail can destroy an entire season's crop in a matter of minutes, literally crushing the grain under a mantle of luxurious, but deadly, white stuff.

The refugee situation here precludes *Ngagpa-la*'s role as protector of the crops since farming is no longer a source of livelihood. His main function now as official weatherman is to keep the weather from turning inclement when special events are being held.

Ngagpa-la has the most unlikely presentation of self for an individual so empowered with holding Himalayan storms at bay. With a body slightly larger than his frame prescribes and a childlike clarity of expression revealing wonderment at even the most mundane things, *Ngagpa-la* is in many respects my idea of the Tibetan teddy bear.

Ngagpa-la seems to be always out and about in this tiny town; one sees him everywhere. After our formal introduction we would often meet along the road and exchange handshakes, chuckles and smiles.

All this non-verbal contact made up for our lack of linguistic communication. He speaks no English; I, broken Tibetan. What's more, he is somewhat hard of hearing. The little language we did exchange often met with this added barrier. Nevertheless, we managed to communicate adequately.

More often than not our brief conversations would turn toward the weather. One day I encountered *Ngagpa-la* on the high Drama Society road during a particularly heavy thunderstorm. He was almost hidden below his big, black umbrella.

Yelling above the rainy din so that he could hear me, I enunciated in my best Tibetan, *"Ngagpa-la, namshe druksha duge?"* ("The weather is lousy, isn't it?"). *"Mare, yakpo du"* ("No, it's good"), he replied, grinning and gesturing up toward the churning mist with a grandiose flourish of his arm. I understood immediately what his simple reply meant. His role was to hold back the clouds only when absolutely necessary. At other times it was essential that the weather be allowed to rebalance itself in order to vent its potential energy and satisfy the gods of the weather.

Still, the image of this modest but powerful weatherman to the Dalai Lama under an umbrella struck me as strangely incongruous.

During my stay in Dharamsala, *Ngagpa-la*'s main services were rendered during the busy New Year and Uprising Day observance period spanning February and March.

The Tibetan New Year of 1979 was preceded by many days of terribly inclement weather. Yet the morning of the first day of the celebrations saw the appearance of blue and sunny skies.

The placid weather continued for the duration of the observance. And, as if by clockwork, after the last day had passed, conditions swung back into eight days of impossibly cold, gray and stormy weather. What a week! It seemed as if the world were coming to an end.

Eight days of terrible weather were about all one could tolerate. But, as if on cue on the morning of March 10, the day Tibetans in exile remember the 1959 resistance to the Chinese takeover of their country, the weather turned crystal clear once again. The Dalai Lama would have perfect weather for his speech before eight thousand Tibetans, foreign press and friends.

The success of both these events rested heavily on *Ngagpa-la*'s shoulders. Every *ngagpa* knows the story of the unfortunate weatherman who failed to prevent hail from destroying the flower garden of the Dalai Lama. Thus, at the March 10th convocation, *Ngagpa-la* stood beaming, self-satisfied, in front of the Tibetan Library. He proudly strolled about, keeping customary watch behind the official tents of His Holiness and lay and monastic officials, human femur horn in hand. His obvious good humor was fueled even further, it seemed, by requests from admirers to take his

72

picture. *Ngagpa-la* stood there aflame in his bright red and orange robes, wrapped in his *ngagpa*'s badge of office, a beige and purple Bhutanese shawl. He cut an ambiguously striking figure, half ancient shaman, half grandfatherly teddy bear. Seeing him at work, however, countered any thoughts of his being just a plain old guy.

Yeshe Dorje is a *tulku*, a highly evolved reincarnated consciousness. Having received esoteric teachings from the old sect of Tibetan Buddhism, the *Nyingma*, he has been trained in the process of exorcism and propitiation of spirits and gods.

I had an opportunity to witness his work directly when he was hired by the Tibetan Music, Dance and Drama Society to straighten out the weather during the performance of a Tibetan opera. Operas are held under a partial tent but the audience is fully exposed. It is critical, therefore, that the weather be clement for the eight-hour-long performances.

In the middle afternoon, during the opera *Pema Woebar*, clouds began to form, obscuring at first the snow-covered rocky peaks and then, to our dismay, the lower pine- and rhododendron-covered ridges immediately above the Drama Society. Such conditions inevitably signal rain during this season.

Perhaps because I was half expecting it, my ear picked out the dim tattoo of a horn peeping out over the songs and percussion instruments from somewhere behind the dining hall. Sure enough, there was *Ngagpa-la*, but today he wasn't posing. He was pointing his horn significantly up towards the menacing cloud cover. Between blasts on the *kan dung* and spells and prayers, he would periodically yell out, *"dro! dro!"* ("Go! Go!"), to the gods of the storm.

Within minutes an interesting thing happened. The clouds stood still.

I could gauge their relative movement by comparing their leading edge in relation to the end of the canvas tent suspended just above myself and my tape recorder. Except for a few moments of random raindrops the arena remained dry, the white clouds hovering just out of range of the opera performance ground.

Whereas I have always been willing to accept something as existing until proven not to exist, I nevertheless temper my optimism with a note of cynicism. But now I had become a confirmed believer.

My newly acquired belief in *Ngagpa-la* was reinforced several days later. Those days began the period when the Dalai Lama gave public teachings in the courtyard between his palace and the temple as part of *Monlam*, the Great Prayer Festival.

It was Friday morning, March 16, and the weather became threatening. Thick clouds began to gather about the mountaintops. It looked as if the glorious weather of the preceding week had gone the way of all things impermanent. Yet, by noon, scarcely one hour before the teachings were about to begin, the weather had cleared into a blue, jeweled sky crowned in sunshine.

So it was to be for the next several days: rain in the mountains, but not on the sacred hill; clearing before and clouding at the teachings' close as if on cue.

Thank you, *Ngagpa-la*.

A Walk with Padmasambhava

The tantric master Padmasambhava, founder of Buddhism in Tibet, journeyed to the present-day Indian village of Rewalsar. There he meditated in a cave high over a massive valley, and took one of the local king's daughters as his consort. The king of Zahor, being angered by his daughter's uncomely behavior, condemned Padmasambhava to be burned alive. The fire was ignited but he was not even scorched. And the flames, turning into water, overspilled to form a beautiful oval lake which Tibetans call *Tsopema*, the Lotus Lake.

Along this stretch of mountain trail, the lake is hidden from view. The hubbub attending the ceremonies and monastic masked dances of the *Nyingma* temple far below on its shores is gone, soaked up by the starkly barren, eroded hills. Wind, cow bells, birds and occasional laughter of Indian hill-women are the only sounds to be heard.

The valley seems to extend infinitely outward from this point two-thirds of the way up the mountainside. It seems to possess a strangely beautiful, yet terrifying power. It beckons, compels, but must be taken carefully, seriously and in measured doses.

This is a land of extremes. Its abrading rockiness, dazzling sunlight and deep crevices make it most appropriately the land that nurtured the power-wielding personality of Padmasambhava. If the land one chooses to live in reflects something of one's thoughts, then this land must have reminded the great *Guru Rinpoche* of the powerful possibilities inherent in the mind. It surely had given him the added strength, during his meditations, to become the great tantric master of the Himalayas. Among these arid hills, under dry blue skies, the *guru* isolated himself in a mountain cave for long periods of retreat.

I have just passed through that cave, past the golden statues of deities, under low hanging rocky clefts and into an open cavern. A huge, glaring statue of the *guru* himself sits carved into eighteen feet of gilded rock. A *dorje* (thunderbolt-scepter) is held incisively in one hand, skull staff in the other. Huge eyes pierce one with the legendary power he manifested to the independent mountain people to the north, powerful enough to consolidate their beliefs and enlist their native gods into a distinctively Tibetan form of Buddhism.

Khatags are everywhere; so too offerings of money. Burning incense sticks punctuate the airways to complete the spectrum of offerings by pilgrims who had made the arduous climb to the top of this ridge. They make the climb to enter physically and spiritually into communion with the essence of this man of power and knowledge. Indeed, for many Tibetans, *Guru Rinpoche* holds more intimate sway over their lives than *Chenrezi*, patron deity of Tibet, or even the Buddha himself.

Perhaps this is because Padmasambhava symbolizes the ordinary man having attained phenomenal heights of personal power and mental development. Perhaps too, his tantric practices did not appear particularly exotic — as they do to us — to the already spirit- and power-oriented Tibetan mountain folk.

Sitting, now, at the top of this mountain, the long-distance panorama reveals the scene upon which the *guru* cast his gaze during his long stay here over a thousand years ago. The Himalayas appear as a long, white, jaggedly-awesome backbone of rock. They are

Padmasambhava, the Buddhist tantric master from the Himalayan foothills of Swat (near the India-Pakistan border), brought Buddhism to Tibet. He accomplished this by vying with the indigenous priests, gods and spirits in feats of magic and spiritual power.

a wall blocking out Tibet from the steamy lowlands beyond. At this moment their magnitude cannot fail to bring to one's mind the natural metaphor of attaining equally lofty spiritual and mental heights. The dry rock, precipitous cliffs and barren soil, relieved by occasional patches of green, lie distantly below, fading into a haze of soft browns and greens.

A tiny *Tsopema* lake, the watery miracle of the *guru*, is again visible here at the top. Only an occasional glint from the gold roofs of temples along its shores suggest ordinary human presence in a land otherwise an abode of yogis, spirits and gods.

Up here caves and rock shelters serve as dwellings for Buddhist meditators. Some have been here for more than fifteen years. Their dwellings dot the rock-strewn slopes. Their residents' only concessions to the works of man are flattened oil-tin roofs extending outward from the rock face, and a personal item or two technologically made.

Prayer flags fly everywhere. Brilliant colors and printed prayers on cloth are set against gray stone, white peaks, and blue sky. They suggest a powerful faith, one set firmly into the earth but extending outward into the far ranges of eternity.

The land of Padmasambhava lies all along this strange beautiful stretch of mountain backbone. And his thoughts and deeds resound through the voices of generations who have made these heights their home.

Milarepa, the beloved eleventh century yogi-poet saint of the Kargyu order of Tibetan Buddhism. Having renounced the ordinary life after dabbling in powerful, magical forces, Milarepa retired to mountain caves where he meditated toward the goal of enlightenment in one single lifetime, subsisting solely on nettles. During his long years of retreat he took students and spread his wisdom through the medium of poetry and song.

Part IV Rites

A Most Singular Breakfast

I had a most singular breakfast this morning. It began when the Last Chance Tea Shop closed owing to a lack of milk, an essential ingredient in tea in this part of the world. It seems the Indian villagers who normally supply it were snowbound farther up the valley.

Out of desperation I decided to try Pema's restaurant, actually a private home. I found it at the end of a dank, seemingly endless, cobblestoned alley, which finally opened onto a pleasant patio overlooking the Kangra Valley.

I entered what appeared to be the archetypal Tibetan, all-purpose sitting/dining room, one of great practicality. A semicircle of three single-bed-sized benches enclosed a table. Morning light streamed in through the two walls of glass windows facing east and south. A three-by-six-foot Tibetan carpet fit perfectly onto each bench allowing two persons to sit very comfortably in the cross-legged Tibetan style, or one person to recline and sleep.

While the room, its furnishings, and the delicious meal of fresh eggs, tea, and excellent brown bread were memorable, what particularly captured my attention was the free "entertainment" taking place in the adjoining room.

A household *puja* was in progress at Pema's. Half a dozen monks were present. These *pujas* have several uses. Some serve to cure a person of a spirit illness, the unfortunate attack of unhealthy spirits. Many more

Masked "hunters" must ritually purify the opera arena before the performance can commence. Tenzing Gompo wears his mask. (Chang)

Sonam Chöden portrays the heroine in the opera Sukyi Nyima, *presented by the Tibetan Institute of Performing Arts. (Chang)*

The young king threatens suicide over love for Sukyi Nyima. *Left to right: Tenzing Gompo (the hermit saint), Tashi Dhöndup (the young king) and Norbu Tsering (the king's hunter). (Chang)*

80

are periodic general housecleanings of unwanted spirit guests and misfortunes.

Tibetans live extraordinarily attuned to the potentially negative forces around them. Rather than wallowing in pessimism or remorse, however, they turn this awareness into lessons in positive living. Acknowledging the potential harm that abounds makes them thankful for the good fortune and simple pleasures that become available with a little mindful effort. Indeed, the Dalai Lama has observed on a number of occasions that it is our enemies, not our friends, who are our most cherished teachers.

Here at Pema's, the monks' deep-voiced chants, *mantras*, clanging bells, swaying thunderbolt-scepters, booming drums, and offerings of flowers, incense and *torma* sculptures, intercede on behalf of the householders in the world of the gods and spirits, to rebalance and re-center the family within the scheme of things. The entire town rings daily from its many windows and doorways with this reassuring sound.

Never before have I had a more enjoyable and enlightening breakfast.

Ama-la *pours out a first glass of New Year's* chang, *the potent alcoholic beverage of Tibet. (Chang)*

As solidly as his image is carved into stone, so did Padmasambhava carve out a place for Buddhism in Tibet. (A Walk with Padmasambhava)

Lama Yeshe Dorje, accomplished tantric master, staves off the rainclouds with blasts on his human femur horn. (The Weatherman, Weather or Not)

Prayer flags of the five customary colors flutter from rooftops to nearby trees. (Green and Red and White and Yellow and Blue Is the Color)

Bringing in the New Year

The New Year must be borne decisively from out of the ashes of the old. Negative thoughts, deeds, and misfortunes accumulated during the previous year are purged from community, home, and individual lives through prescribed rituals by clergy and members of the household.

The ushering in of *losar*, the New Year, begins on the evening of the twenty-ninth day of the last month of the old year. Tibetan friends and family gather together to partake of *gutuk*, the "special nine soups." Contained within are sculpted and stuffed dumplings, which signify the fortunes for the coming year of every person present. The person who chooses a dumpling stuffed with salt might gain renown and lead a virtuous life during the coming twelve moons. Whoever gets the chili pepper will be angry and argumentative. And woe be it to he or she with the lump of charcoal, for that person will be cursed with a black heart. This provides many laughs for most and frowns for a few.

Each person finishes all but a little of his soup. The leftovers, along with old food, coins, pieces of clothing lint, a candle, and a *khatag* greeting-scarf are put together into a large bowl along with a humanoid-shaped *torma* sculpture known as *lu*. These serve as ransom offerings to attract the accrued evil and misfortune of the past year away from the household. The men carry the items to a lonely spot along the road by torchlight, crying "Come out! Come out!" to the evils.

Discovering the contents of one's "special nine soups" divination dumpling at the end of the old year is an occasion for smiles and sometimes for frowns. The article enclosed within the soup dumpling foretells one's fortune for the coming year.

The job done, they quickly return without ever looking back, for to do so would cause the evil to return with them. This act, it occurs to me, is a powerful metaphor to a central notion in the Tibetan experience, that one must continue on life's path without looking back. "No attachments, no regrets," a lama once observed.

On the afternoon of the twenty-ninth day, the main temple comes alive with chanting and praying, punctuated with the tattoos of twelve-foot long silver and gold horns that one can feel as well as hear. These add a filigree ground to the vocal devotionals and to the velvet throb of the drums, themselves looking like circular world planes, like wheels of the *dharma*, and particularly like the drums the old shamans' souls used for riding into the sky. Aided by the staccato wings of the cymbals, the vocal prayers are lifted into the mountains hovering above the temple. These sounds seem

83

to add the necessary power surge for carrying evil spirits and misfortunes up and away from the community.

Prayers continue, and soon a procession of monks and lamas quits the temple. They carry with them special New Year *zor tormas*, huge constructions embodying the placated evils accrued by the community during the past year. Skull-like death's heads top these conical sculptures, which are sometimes adorned with sausage-like entrails, nude human male and female likenesses, flames, and other signs imbued with the suggestion of our earthly misdeeds, frustrations, and misfortunes. Like the household *lü* offerings, these contain accumulated negativities, which over the past several days have been enticed into their elaborate forms through the ritual prayers and the combined will of the assembled clergy.

When the proper moment arrives, the *torma* is paraded down the hill to a large straw mound, the pyre on

Casting out the lü *ransom effigy on the twenty-ninth night of the last month of the old year. The men carry it to a lonely spot with the cries, "Come out! Come out!" to entice the evils away from the family and household.*

which the physical manifestations of the evil will be burned, taking them out of harm's way.

More prayers and instrumental sound are offered. When the *torma* is finally thrown into the hollow of the straw mound it is done with marked fervor. One never sees monks move with such deliberately coarse actions as when they rudely throw our accumulated evils into the straw pyre. It is then quickly set ablaze while sanctified water is poured in a circular path before the inferno. The water-that-cuts-fire protects us from the possibility of the evil escaping back upon us.

One *losar*, I attended the *torma* burning with a Tibetan companion. I knew that for him this event came at a particularly fateful time. His baby son was in danger of dying of an affliction attended by partial paralysis. The lamas said it was not curable by medicine. They explained that it was a karmic affliction, the onslaught of malevolent spirit forces, which cannot be seen or controlled by ordinary persons.

Holding each other's hand we rushed off, away from the crackling and exploding inferno, and I knew that somewhere in his thoughts was the hope that this communal cleansing could help the baby as well.

Today's casting out of the *zor torma* is over. What in the past few days had been eager expectation brimming with potential energy is now erupting into visual and aural pyrotechnics. I do not think that I had ever truly known the real meaning of a fireworks free-for-all until this evening. Firecrackers, rockets, bombs, sparklers had always been fun to play with. But tonight I understand the deeper meaning in it all. We aren't lighting them up for the sheer excitement alone. We are commemorating the chance to experience, once more, the cleansed soul of the child. The New Year is truly a time of renewal of body, mind and spirit.

Right now, things are getting quite exciting outside. A particularly powerful explosion shattered the semi-silence just a second ago, and I am beginning to feel the call of the wild. I've got these three skyrockets here beside me on the bed. Excuse me, please, while I go up on the roof and set them off over the Kangra Valley.

(Ten minutes later) Ah, that was great fun. You know, I'd always felt a little self-conscious setting off fireworks back home, perhaps because I'd never really felt a good reason for doing so.

(Twenty minutes later) Is nothing sacred? They're setting off rockets and fireworks from the *stupa*. It's perfectly dangerous here in town. Oh well, as a lama friend once sarcastically observed, "What the hell, you only live once!"

New Year, New Thoughts

To the Buddhist way of thinking, our misfortunes and frustrations result from the negative thoughts and deeds that we have created during this and previous lifetimes. Accordingly, when Tibetans participate in the *losar* observance, they mark more than the arrival of a new year. They recognize the passing of twelve lunar months full of thoughts and deeds.

Along with the discarded *zor torma* go the attachments and negativities of the previous year. For *losar* gives Tibetans the opportunity to both contemplate the past and to mark out a more sunny road ahead during the coming year.

In the West, the arrival of the new year provides an opportunity for rejoicing and making resolutions for the coming year. But unlike the Tibetan, our new year observance no longer carries with it the belief and conviction that insure that the new year will provide a true renewal of spirit or a change in the circumstances of living.

Tibetans are taught from infancy to be mindful of their own actions, especially as they affect others. Through this careful attention toward their deeds, and the symbolic purging of unbeneficial thoughts and actions at the new year time, Tibetans effectively turn their energies toward building a better coming year.

The beginning of this new year was marked by the customary public blessing by the Dalai Lama. Tibetans from all over India, Nepal, and places even more remote, began arriving in Dharamsala several days before the commencement of *losar*. Their purpose for being here at this time revolved about the event of going into the palace grounds to be physically blessed by His Holiness. The Dalai Lama is, after all, considered the earthly embodiment of the Buddha's quality of boundless compassion. As the incarnation of the *bodhisattva Avalokiteshvara* (*Chenrezi* in Tibetan), he was offering to each pilgrim a powerful initial momentum toward a positive and successful year.

The mood of the people awaiting his blessing on this second day of the year imparted to me a special kind of excitement. A line of people had begun to form along the road leading to the temple and palace grounds during the wee hours of the morning. Their special holiday dress revealed their regional diver-

Special new year's display consisting of (left section, top to bottom): fruit; desi, a sweet ceremonial rice dish; chang; the triple gem signifying the Buddha, the religion and the clergy; coral tree; (center) box of barley kernals on the left and chemar in the right compartment, both used as a wish for good luck; bags of money, silver, gold, rice, butter, cheese and barley; cloth; tea bricks; (right) sacred water vase; flower; desi; ivory tusks; and mirror of crystalline consciousness.

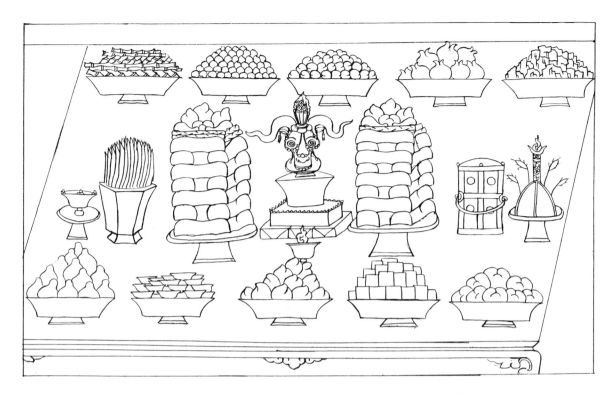

Special new year's display consisting of fruit and sweets (top and bottom rows) and symbolic foods (middle row) including (left to right): "first chang," grain beer; "first growth," barley shoots signifying successful agriculture; kapse, special new year's pastry; lungpo, butter sheep's head signifying successful herding; kapse, "first curd," the best curd from yak or goat milk; and chemar, the mixture of roasted barley flour, butter and sugar used to wish all a happy and fortunate new year.

sity, relative wealth and status, as well as the degree of importance that they placed on this part of the observance.

Many wore family heirlooms. Gold, turquoise and coral glinted from ears, necks and fingers. Some clothing was old: handmade, homespun, brightly colored, open-hearted garments, carried across the Himalayas from Tibet. Many clothes were newly-made; at *losar* time the renewal of the year is echoed in the desire to wear something entirely new. New blouses, women's dresses, men's cloaks, shirts and shoes make their *début*. However, the fine older garments also convey the feeling of renewal due to the infrequency of their use.

The old folks wore the more loosely fitting silk and woolen styles. The younger men wore modern polyester and cotton blended *chuba* cloaks with western shirts, while the young women stood out, doll-like in more contoured styles.

Tibetans do not fit the stereotype of the polite and self-effacing Asian; as such they are not very good at standing docilely in line. Considering accounts from previous years, I and my companions were quite surprised that during this past hour the people were able to contain their excitement and remain even momentarily in line. But as you know, when you're boiling milk, the pot is bound to overflow. And a portion of the crowd soon plunged ecstatically ahead of us.

Western propriety surged momentarily into our minds. "Why, after all, should they sneak ahead of us?" we thought. But smiles immediately replaced the anger as we too became caught up in the mood of hopeful anticipation and excitement at getting blessed by the living Buddha. Everyone needs a little hope in their lives, and once a year, if not every day, there should be a time for celebrating it. Plants need sun. People need hope. The Tibetans brought to His Holiness's palace grounds an exuberant anticipation, and a compelling energy that attracted more of the same. Tibetans from all regions and lifestyles and a number of Westerners like ourselves (also dressed in traditional Tibetan garb), were buzzing like live wires blowing in a gale.

The line snaked down the ridge road past the old codger chipping mantras into slate tabs, and ultimately up to the temple-monastery complex.

The pace was quickening now as people surged up the ramp in to the temple grounds proper. The lines opened up into a courtyard. Trees pregnant with purple buds eager to bloom adorned the stone walks as men and women were separated into orderly lines. The realities of life in this world made it necessary that each pilgrim be body-searched before entering into direct physical contact with the precious spiritual leader of six million Tibetans.

On a less urgent level, the lines were needed to insure proper decorum, so important in this part of the world.

His Holiness the Fourteenth Dalai Lama gives his blessings during the first days of the new year. His tutors and other high lamas stand about his throne. Government officials sit to the Dalai Lama's right. One official is offering him a khatag. *Behind him in line are others bearing gifts and desiring blessings. These include Tibetans from various regions of the country, a Mongol, an Indian, a Nepali, and even a Muslim.*

The requisites of security and propriety done, we were admitted into quite literally another world.

The ambience of the palace grounds was one of great serenity, the more apparent in comparison with the crowd's excited maneuvering outside the gates.

To preserve this feeling a single file was established. The line contained old and young, Tibetan and Westerner, those traditionally-clad and those in everyday dress. All had white *khatags* draped around their necks as offerings to His Holiness.

During the final approach, the line swung into a wide arc about fifty feet from the Dalai Lama. Within a moment of noting the Dalai Lama touching the bowed heads of a group of Tibetans, Dale and I realized that he had made eye contact with us, first through that intense glint of eye and then a broad smile.

When my turn came to be blessed, instead of the touch upon the temples given to Tibetans, I received the more Western handshake. The Dalai Lama's smile and laugh, a deep guffaw so reminiscent of his elder brother's, which I'd had the occasion to hear many times in America, infected me with joy. Indeed, it was as if he seemed glad at my presence — all the more, it seemed, because of my Tibetan dress at which he gleefully remarked, fingering the sleeve of my *chuba*, "Ah, Tibetan dress!" Unmonumental as that response would seem, I had received that for which I had come.

To the Long Life of the Dalai Lama

Slowly — deliberately —

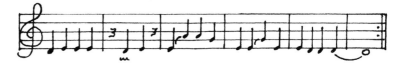

The chant lingers, a sinuous thought working itself wormlike into the deepest reaches of the mind. Here at the *puja* dedicated to preserving a long life for the Dalai Lama I sit on the floor of the balcony of the temple amid hundreds of Tibetans. Inside the temple scores of monks, lamas and His Holiness himself, swaying on his silken throne, intone the chant.

Once again I experience that almost unnerving, indescribable energy that seems to emanate from these devout people whenever the Dalai Lama is near. It is as if a mild static electricity permeates the air, as in those few moments before the thunderstorm, when several hours of dull uneasiness yield to a dramatic exhilaration of body and spirit.

The people from Amdo are offering this particularly elaborate *puja*. Being from the same region of Tibet as is this Dalai Lama, they are quite proud of their origin and consider this a solemn matter.

What is beginning to unfold at this early-morning gathering is both a dramatic enactment, reinforcing the importance of the Dalai Lama to his people, and a serious religious act to prevent evil, illness or misfortune from taking him away.

A huge stack of *kapse*, pastry, biscuits and fruit has been carefully arranged into a massive pile before the main entrance of the temple. Sheltered under an orange tent ablaze with the symbol of the eternal knot, these offerings to the gods are ways of buying more time for the Dalai Lama.

Tibetans believe that the Dalai Lama will remain here in his present body, and then take rebirth indefinitely, as long as he is kept from inordinate negative influences and feels able to work effectively on behalf of his people and all other sentient beings. Thus the Amdo folk arranged this elaborate plea for his continued help and as a spiritual prophylaxis on his behalf.

As I sit by trying to soak in all the sights and sounds, a Tibetan acquaintance has just grabbed my arm and is pointing excitedly in the direction of the temple doors. There stand five young monks dressed in tantric yogi outfits impersonating *dakinis*, the female messengers of the Buddha realm, known in Tibetan as *khadoma* (sky-goers). They have come here to ask the Dalai Lama to return to the Buddha field, the realm, or more precisely the state of mind and being, outside the endless spiral of birth, death and rebirth characterizing this world of suffering and illusion. Being the emanation of the compassionate aspect of the Buddha's mind, he is considered able to consciously leave his body and rejoin them in Buddha field at will. In counterpoint to the *dakinis'* requests are the chants and prayers of the assembled monks and lay persons asking him to remain.

The dilemma then is: what can be done to satisfy both sides concerned? The answer lies in compromise through substitution. As one lama explained, "Instead of giving the *dakinis* the Dalai Lama, we give them his representation in the form of a statue." Another lama put it this way, "In order to keep hold of 100 rupees, we give away ten."

The messengers from the Buddha field are being

The double dorje *consists of two crossed "thunder-bolt" scepters. The* dorje *is one of the two basic hand implements used in ritual. It embodies the male principle which, in turn, signifies the aspect of method. The other implement is the hand bell. This embodies the female principle of wisdom. Together they provide the means of skilfully attaining enlightenment. The Tibetan story of creation tells of the universe being formed out of a giant double* dorje *made from solidified wind. The double* dorje *is considered a symbol of stability and is hung on lamas' thrones*

asked to make an even greater sacrifice. They are being entreated to carry away with them all the obstacles to his health and success. Tibetans reason that if the *dakinis* really love him then they will take away his troubles instead of his presence.

Another lama once explained the method of gathering together the evil obstacles. He calls the devices that are used, "trouble trappers." These may take a number of forms, but today one of the most dramatic and ancient forms is being employed. The troublesome and potentially evil spirit obstacles are strongly cajoled through prayer and chant to accept the hospitality of the Tibetans in the form of a beautiful palace. It is made of *namkhas*, elaborate thread cross constructions of geometrically shaped concentric bands of color resolving into a central "eye." Today's palace for the obstacles is a particularly elaborate one consisting of a colored thread parasol towering over numerous multi-colored diamond-shaped *namkhas* and various *torma* offerings. These appear very beautiful to the obstacles. The *mandala*-like *namkhas* attract the attention of the evil forces, diverting them from the Dalai Lama. This outer palace complements an inner palace created by the visualizations of the monks. Thus seduced, the evils enter their new home, and its doors are sealed, locking in the obstacles through more visualizations and prayers.

The *dakinis*, having acceded to the entreaties of the people pick up their "ten rupee statue" and the *namkha* palace. They carry these out to a waiting truck with a good deal of urgency. There had been a marked tension in the air prior to the exit of the offerings. With the procession now out of sight there has arisen a lightness, even a giddiness in my mind, and so too, it seems in many of those sitting around me.

Into the truck go the things. They and their bearers are now traveling, we are told, to Pathankot, four hours away. There after taking great pains not to look back

Dakinis (*known in Tibetan as* khadoma, *"sky goer") are the fairy-like messengers from the Buddha realm.*

during their journey, as this would void the spiritual contract and reverse the effect of the ceremony, the *dakinis* will dispose of the offerings into a large lake.

The disposal of such anti-offerings is prescribed in the ritual texts. Sometimes fire is indicated, as in the expulsion of the misfortune-laden *zor torma* at New Year's time. Sometimes simply leaving it out by a crossroads is all that is necessary. There, the evils will choose one of many paths whereby to exit the scene.

The disposal by water suggests that some of the obstacles are associated with water and are probably *lü*, or *nagas*, the generally-feared and always-to-be-placated scorpion, frog or snake-like spirits. These underworld creatures will receive the ransoms offered in place of the Dalai Lama at the biggest body of water in the area. They are borne there by the *dakini* messengers in the hope that an ounce of prevention is worth a pound of cure.

To one lama, these offerings will continue to do good in their new surroundings. As Tibetans are concerned with establishing harmony between themselves and the spirits, gods, and other sentient beings co-existing in the universe, the ransoms not only satisfy, they benefit those few *lü* in the lake who would wish to "seek help from the Buddhist teachings." There exist good beings even in the lesser realms of *samsara*; and these will benefit from the consecrated offerings.

The *dakini*-monks will remain away from Dharamsala for one week. Thereafter, spiritually cleansed, they will return not as celestial messengers but as voluntary bearers of the misfortunes of the Dalai Lama. They will bring, as well, renewed hopes for the continued happiness and prosperity of the Tibetan people.

A female underwater spirit, known as lü *or* naga. *She manifests most commonly as a snake. Here she is depicted offering a wish-fulfilling gem as a gift to a Buddha.*

The Dalai Lama at the Kalachakra initiation, Madison, Wisconsin, 1981. (Eastern Winds over Western Fields)

Conical piles of white crystalline rocks are physical evidence of the intense spiritual contract comprising an offering to the deities. (Offering)

Tibetan women perform the old songs and round dances in their best dress. (New Year, New Thoughts)

A Tibetan villager (foreground) listens spellbound to the words of the Dalai Lama. (At a Teaching by the Dalai Lama)

Misdeeds, misthoughts and misfortunes of the old year are attracted to the skull-topped torma. A monk awaits the signal to carry it to its fiery end. (Bringing in the New Year)

Part V Musing

To fanfare of drums, cymbals, horns and chants, the New Year tormas await immolation, marking the advent of the New Year. (Bringing in the New Year)

Sunrise over the Himalayas. (The Sun Upon its Rounds)

Offering

Making an offering is entering into a spiritual contract. In making an offering one affirms that unseen forms of sentience and power pervade the phenomenal world and may be brought into focus for the individual by this concerted act of faith.

Offerings are objects transformed by the appropriate mental attitude. The stone incised with an ancient script becomes an aspect of the Buddha. Even a lock of hair, piece of blessed string, bough of juniper needles, or sparkling piece of rock can take on the role of messenger between the individual spirit of the offerant and a spiritual representative of the greater reservoir beyond.

The offering may be a tangible object, but prayer, song, or thought will do equally well. More often than not, however, people need to offer up the easily seen in order to reassure themselves of effectively entering into touch with the infinite. Little wonder that, worldwide, people offer up fragrant smoke, special stones, vigorous fire, and beautiful flowers.

For some, a simple gift will suffice. For others, the finer and more elaborate the offering, the firmer the foundation of their belief. In the end, it matters little what one gives. True sincerity and motivation of belief ultimately attain the desired effect.

Belief, borne either from mere acceptance or through critical examination, enlivens the act of offering, enabling the gift to become a live conductor between the

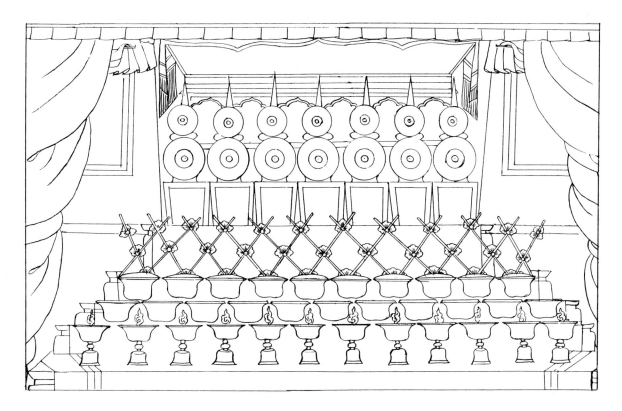

A large offering altar consisting of (top to bottom) torma *(ritual food for the deities or spirits); incense sticks with tree seed "flowers"; and butter lamps.*

individual fragment and the totality. Giving becomes receiving.

For a blissfully intense moment we connect. All that most of us can ever hope for is that rare instant during which the heart's mind does the dance the brain's mind never quite learns to master. By giving offerings through the partnership of the senses and the will one is transported momentarily away from habitual attention to the self toward the Buddha-like feeling of clean and simple being.

The Sun upon its Rounds

Having taken a seat on this rhododendron- and pine-covered hillside, I look forward to basking in the golden rays of the setting sun.

This is a time of repose, of meditative solitude. This is a time when people who live according to the diurnal rhythms of sun and moon, and blinding light and subtle darkness, take their rest. This is that special time which is nature's way of offering her reward for a day's living well done.

The peacefulness at sunset is a marker by which living things put their bodies and spirits at rest. The time elapsed between the sun's rising and setting is, for each season, exactly and perfectly the appropriate amount of time in which the organism can effectively act. As the sun rises it emerges from rest, and soon after sunset slides into rest. And I reflect how Tibetan monks, *ama-las*, nomads, farmers, indeed all the people of the world living by natural time, must be so much the better for it.

The sun also serves as a powerful philosophical metaphor. It calls up through its daily movement the inescapable message of our brief lifetimes on this earth. We are born, like the sun, seemingly from nowhere. We grow, we act, affecting others in our path. We shine brilliantly through our early days, although sometimes finding our radiance hidden by life's clouds which, at times, enter our field of view.

Our inner light grows, often despite ourselves. At

life's midday, its powerful beacon illuminates every nook and cranny in our immediate world. And it seems that we shall remain here forever, exploring and tasting everything in the glow.

But as the sunlight turns to amber it begins to dawn upon us that the shadows we now cast have grown longer. With them, familiar events, people and objects take on yet another view, indeed have taken on numerous views throughout the course of our lives. Like the sun, the grand metaphor, we ultimately begin to ebb in light and warmth. Finally, when life sets and death comes, our spirits are released beyond the western hills.

But as the sun sets inexorably over successive western hills, it also rises continually over successive eastern horizons. And this is where the crux of the problem lies. As the rays of the sun, so too go our spirits? Will our consciousnesses indeed come again, after their courses are run through the night-time world of the death passage?

For Tibetan Buddhists the return is not in question. It is inevitable and eternal until compassionate personal enlightenment is attained. What is striven for is not rebirth, but liberation from the rounds of birth, death, and ensuing rebirth. The goal is not to become subject to the cycles of day and night, but to become in one's self as the sun, a steady source of beneficient light.

(Ten minutes later) As I sat on that mountainside, face warming in the golden glow and mind considering the sun as a metaphor to enlightenment, a horn blared out in the vicinity of the temple and monastery. At first, my fantasy-charged mind imagined the Dalai Lama's weatherman, Yeshe Dorje, to be blowing his thigh-bone horn, forestalling a coming storm or ritually heralding the sinking sun.

I rose and set off in the direction of the sound. There, on a promontory overlooking the Kangra Valley crouched a young monk blowing a metal horn towards the rock faces and hidden mountain valleys. For each tattoo he produced he received a faithful response, only more ephemeral, as the remote mountain vastnesses themselves. His horn sent out shimmering blasts a quarter-tone apart, with even more subtle sliding pitches in between. And he colored them with the full range of dynamics, a loud staccato would melt into quiet meditational hums and would slide, once more, into a blinding blare.

After twenty minutes he quit his perch and having met my glance came over to say hello. The young monk's upper lip had temporarily formed into the shape of a nipple from the mouthpiece of the horn. The horn itself was a work of extreme beauty; beaten out of solid silver it was wrapped with silver wire and decorated along its bell with human skulls, reminders of our impermanence.

"Do you do this everyday?" I asked, hoping to tape record him at a later date. "No, only once in a while," he answered. "I'm practicing, you see. I play this at *pujas*, and I need to be practiced for them."

What an ideal way of practicing an instrument, bouncing sounds off snow-capped mountains half-shrouded in mist and bathed in sun-setting light. Perhaps this was his only time for practice. Somehow though, I think the moment he had chosen was not solely one of convenience.

He was speaking out to the rocky crags; calling out to the spirits and gods inhabiting them, toasting them; calling out to the snow lions, lauding them with sounds as swift as their leaps from one peak to the next; calling out to the infinite out there, and likewise within, with sublime offerings in the form of sound.

Secrets of the Mountain Fog

If lowland fog slips in quietly on cats' feet, then mountain fog is a lion by comparison. It boils and churns up the gorge between mountain foothills. It envelops the homes and prayer flags of the Tibetans of Dharamsala, at times hiding the tiny community without a trace.

Such fog is alive and I cannot help drawing a parallel between it and *lung*, literally "wind," which Tibetans conceive to be the body's life-bearing circulatory energy. Only, this *lung* courses through a more massive organism, the earth itself.

The mountains are its skin, infinite wrinkles of rocky crags.

Upon each fold of rock exists a smaller universe still, of minute hairs: blood red rhododendron blossoms against a bed of deep green leaves, and rainbow fields of wildflowers.

The glaciers where snow lions leap and play are the whites of its eyes.

Water, life's blood of the earth being, flows from head to foot with a momentum knowing no beginning or end. It returns *ad infinitum* from the ocean's depths to the summits of the well-pronounced goosebumps on the earth's flesh that are the Himalayas.

We, in turn, are the micro-organisms making our way on those bumps of sensitive skin. For the brief moment that we exist (when reckoned in geologic time) we strain eternally to reach the upper levels of the sky. At first we were able only to climb. In this era we fly, rocket-assisted and computer-directed, but in a certain important respect, with closed eyes.

Blinded by our desire to attain the realm of the sun, we often fail to notice that the same radiance glows from within the earth's many jewels: from its waters, flowers, spiders' webs, cats' eyes, and though less visibly, from within our own hearts and minds. They all reflect the same power that we associate with the sun and sky.

The fog slides in brazenly. Unabashedly it cracks the sunlight into infinite miniature suns glowing from each droplet of mist. The countless flowers, crags, trees, flashing wings and darting eyes populating this mountain world play hide and seek with the eyes in the mist. Elusive to the eyes, they appear even more vividly to the mind by their absence in the fog.

Eastern Winds over Western Fields

I had never believed in living according to the whims of fate. I would acknowledge the existence of coincidental events, but quickly explained them away with the rationalization, "Statistically it was bound to happen." To believe that some force external to the participants could be pulling the strings of coincidence chafed my rationalistic mind. This one-sided view was reinforced by the equally rigid attachment of many of my peers to a romantic, supernatural explanation for every event.

My attitude began to change, however, after my first sojourn with the Tibetans. The Tibetan experience provided the proper catalyst to break down my fanatical belief in non-belief, and to shift my orientation to the open-minded middle ground between the two extremes.

I had cast the die that was to put me smack on the path of interconnectedness. Buddhists call this path *karma*, one in which people and things interacting at various times and places cause certain results to occur to all concerned.

Unlike the virtual anarchism of the West, Dharamsala offered an environment in which an action on my part often provided a noticeable and immediate effect upon myself and others. In the West, countless people strive vainly for happiness and success. They act habitually at their own timing and personal whim. Tibetans' lives are premised, on the other hand, more upon the natural intersection of events rather than upon deliberate and idiosyncratic action. Tibetans live within the karmic dimension with the result that coincidence, as we perceive it to be manifest, becomes the rule rather than the exception.

Within weeks of my arrival the need for an explanation for this subtle state of events became almost an obsession. I considered the fact that Dharamsala is, after all, a small town and thus conducive to coincidence. So too are there small towns in the United States, but they lack this special quality. I considered the fact that the population was more homogeneous than its American counterparts. Then again, after some weeks I observed that Dharamsala was home to many Tibetan regional, economic and social subcultures. In fact it represented a grand cross-section of Tibet, a complicated society of people having mutually unintelligible dialects and disparate customs developed by living in isolated mountain valleys, freezing deserts, monasteries and palaces of aristocrats.

Thus Dharamsala was not the archetypal homogenous community — an all too convenient explanation of its well-formed ecology of events. Rather than stop there in my reasoning I was now forced to search into hidden psycho-cultural recesses for the answer.

In Dharamsala, one always seems to encounter the person, object or answer that is needed at the proper moment. The only explanation I could ultimately conjure was that these well-timed conjunctions resulted from being in a society which functioned under the *gestalt* of *karma*.

At its basis, *karma*, the Buddhist version of the ancient dialectical paradigm of cause and effect, recognizes that at some point in timeless time, you and all other sentient beings have affected one another, in various ways have been related to one another. Our present actions are the result of the maturation of the momentum of these relationships, creating a defin-

Woodblock print of the soon-to-be-enlightened Shakyamuni Buddha resisting the forces of Mara, demon of illusion. Mara sends his armies of illusion to conquer Buddha as he sits meditating under the tree of enlightenment. Their arrows, lances, wind, and rain turn to lotuses upon entering the Buddha's mental sphere. Undaunted, Mara sends his three daughters, craving, lust, and discontent, in the form of a virgin, a somewhat experienced beautiful young woman, and a well experienced older woman, to entice him sexually. But to no avail; he is beyond it all.

able tidal flow behind our actions and reactions. Sometimes the effects are not felt for days, years, or as Buddhists believe, lifetimes. Yet the *karma* will eventually come to pass, or "ripen," and the individual consciousness experiences the calm or storm of its previous actions.

Westerners tend to view *karma* as synonymous with fate. Here, fate implies an unbending cast of one's die of destiny. For Tibetans, *karma* is closer to "the state of the system." Some human systems need more power; others need to be cooled off. Some systems need more compassion while others, increased input of intellectual wisdom. Thus, with proper inspection of one's *karma*, one neither abandons oneself to its flow nor ignores it: one puts energy into directing it toward more productive ends.

Tibetans live cognizant of the dynamics that mold their experiences and thoughts. They act to enhance the good through accepting the reality of each person or event, their judgment uncluttered by egocentric projection. Tibetans do not push up river in a speedboat to get to the island; they simply stroll up along the bank, dive in upstream from the island, then float there with the least possible effort.

"They are so intelligent," observed a wise old friend of the Tibetans. This is an intelligence borne not only of the intellect but from accurately sensing the flow and connection of events. It was, no doubt, this worldliness that enabled the Tibetan refugees to recoup so effectively after the tragic loss of their country.

The Tibetans' ability to evaluate and act on experience in a karmic way is most certainly due to their Buddhism, but not completely. Their awareness of the flow of events is, it seems to me, partly the result of their close interaction with the natural world. Seeing the connections among natural events on the wild plateau of Tibet set the stage for accepting so infinite a psychological strategy as Buddhism.

To be aware of the subtle movements, nuances, goodness and horror of nature is in itself a powerful lesson in illusion and impermanence. In Dharamsala, sometimes the snow mountains would hover unmistakeably over the foothills, while at other times I could not be convinced that they existed out there, beyond the clouds and mist walling in the tiny town.

Being well-centered within the earthly world has enabled Tibetans to actively pursue the ethereal religious path. Tibetan religion is, in fact, a complex intermingling of Buddhism — the tantric form imported from India in 700 A.D. — with the even more ancient shamanism of northeast Asia, a view shared with the distant cousin of the Tibetans, the North American Indian.

Tibetan religion expresses an ecology of a universe equally finite to our planet as it is infinite. It personifies the universal forces of nature in the form of a bewildering complexity of deities and spirits of the water, earth, trees, mountains and sky. These act side by side with the Buddhist pantheon, which encapsulates a parallel ecology of mind.

Tibetan religion places primary emphasis upon maintaining harmony in both realms of outer and inner experience. Negative spirit or positive deity are urged to live in harmony with humans and all other sentient entities. Those who refuse are placated, bribed, cajoled, and ultimately compelled to restablish harmonious relations. Likewise, the mental teachings are oriented toward establishing a harmony of mental events.

With experience based in nature, Tibetans already had the mental template and lifestyle conducive to the practice of the karmic way. When the bearers of Buddhism arrived 1,300 years ago with their method for establishing harmony with the gods and demons within one's own mind, they encountered a receptive audience.

Acting with awareness of a natural ecology without

and within balances Tibetans on their journey along the path through life. Perhaps, in the end, it was this attention to maintaining harmony that created the ambience that I experienced in Dharamsala. The Tibetan blithely refers to it as "being lucky." The Westerner, more consciously, seeks it out to improve his "quality of life."

The great seal of the Kalachakra Tantra. *The* Kalachakra *belongs to the highest order of tantric practices. Long and detailed study, elaborate meditative visualizations, and exacting physical yoga are required in order to follow the* Kalachakra *path of mental development. The* Kalachakra *lineage of knowledge is held by the Dalai Lama who, with the aid of certain other lamas, is empowered to initiate and teach it to others. The* Kalachakra *initiation is held infrequently, but a few times in each Dalai Lama's lifetime. The present Dalai Lama has given the initiation more times than most. In July 1981 he initiated fifteen hundred Western Buddhists in a country meadow outside Madison, Wisconsin. This was the first time that it had been held outside Asia. With this event came,* de facto, *official recognition of the advent of Tibetan Buddhism as a serious way of life and thought in the West.*

A Last Word

The sun is rising now over the Himalayan foothills, exploding through the hazy edge between pale blue sky and tree-covered, rocky ridge. It has so risen since the mountains were thrust up out of the primeval ocean by the tectonic forces of the earth. In all these years it has warmed chilly skins and illuminated sleep-filled eyes of countless people fortunate enough to mark the first few moments of their day with this ultimate of timepieces.

Thus begins my first day back in Dharamsala. In the course of a few sunrises I have journeyed directly to the other side of the earth, and have entered literally another world. It is now almost nightfall in North America. Here at the doorstep to the roof of Asia it is dawn.

The sudden transit from one time and place to another is terribly distracting but utterly welcome. Being in another land, culture, and frame of time is a constructive upheaval. It is a rude but inwardly satisfying change from that undefinable ambience back home which accustoms one to accept unimportant circumstances and beliefs as significant, and blinds one from having new and exciting experiences, which consistently slip past in the normal course of living. When one is away from the old habits, old places and old people one becomes renewed. A rebirth of spirit arises.